ISSUES THAT CONCERN YOU

Electronic Devices in Schools

Laurie Willis, *Book Editor*

GREENHAVEN PRESS
A part of Gale, Cengage Learning

GALE
CENGAGE Learning·

Detroit • New York • San Francisco • New Haven, Conn • Waterville, Maine • London

Elizabeth Des Chenes, *Director, Publishing Solutions*

For more information, contact:
Greenhaven Press
27500 Drake Rd.
Farmington Hills, MI 48331-3535
Or you can visit our Internet site at gale.cengage.com

For product information and technology assistance, contact us at

Gale Customer Support, 1-800-877-4253
For permission to use material from this text or product, submit all requests online at www.cengage.com/permissions

Further permissions questions can be e-mailed to permissionrequest@cengage.com

Articles in Greenhaven Press anthologies are often edited for length to meet page requirements. In addition, original titles of these works are changed to clearly present the main thesis and to explicitly indicate the author's opinion. Every effort is made to ensure that Greenhaven Press accurately reflects the original intent of the authors. Every effort has been made to trace the owners of copyrighted material.

Cover image © Goodluz/Shutterstock.com

LIBRARY OF CONGRESS CATALOGING-IN-PUBLICATION DATA

Electronic devices in schools / Laurie Willis, book editor.
    p. cm. -- (Issues that concern you)
  Summary: "Electronic Devices in Schools: This series provides readers with information on topics of current interest. Focusing on important social issues, each anthology examines its subject in a variety of ways, from personal accounts to factual articles"-- Provided by publisher.
  Includes bibliographical references and index.
  ISBN 978-0-7377-6292-1 (hardback)
1. Educational technology. 2. Education--Effect of technological innovations on. 3. Mobile communication systems. I. Willis, Laurie.
  LB1028.3.E4274 2012
  371.33--dc23
                                                                          2012027204

Printed in the United States of America
1 2 3 4 5 6 7 16 15 14 13 12

CONTENTS

Introduction   5

1. Electronic Devices Can Be Useful Learning Tools   8
   Day Rosenberg

2. More Schools Are Encouraging the Use of
   Electronic Devices   15
   Ian Quillen

3. iPods Can Help Students Learn   24
   Kathleen Kennedy Manzo

4. iPads Could Hinder Teaching, Professors Say   29
   Ben Wieder

5. Bring-Your-Own-Laptop Programs Help Education   37
   Jeff Weinstock

6. Bring-Your-Own-Laptop Programs Are
   Complicated but Worthwhile   46
   Eamonn O'Donovan

7. Laptops Should Be Banned from Classrooms   54
   Timothy Snyder

8. Schools Should Ban Cell Phones   59
   Eric Novak

9. Cell Phones Can Be Learning Tools Instead
   of Distractions   64
   William M. Ferriter

10. Texting Is a Distraction from Learning   69
    Patrick Welsh

11. Cell Phones in the Classroom May Lead to
    Secretly Created Videos   74
    Vaishali Honawar

12. Electronic Communication Between Teachers
    and Students Raises Difficult Issues   81
    Katie Ash

Appendix

   What You Should Know About Electronic
   Devices in Schools   88

   What You Should Do About Electronic
   Devices in Schools   90

Organizations to Contact   93

Bibliography   97

Index   99

Picture Credits   104

Highlighting the conflicting views expressed by teachers and school administrators about using electronic devices in the classroom, author and educator Liz Kolb asserts that "it's important to start looking at the cell phone as the Swiss Army knife of learning, rather than the most annoying thing in the classroom."[1] Whether electronic devices are permitted and used constructively in the classroom hinges largely on the attitudes of educators. While all believe in the central goal of giving students a quality education, attitudes vary widely about whether electronic devices in the classroom help or hinder students.

Some, like professor Paul Thagard of the University of Waterloo in Ontario, Canada, believe that "students absorbed in their laptops are not only ineffective in their passive learning strategies, but are also missing out on crucial active and social aspects of learning. . . . Moreover, learning in a classroom should be a social process in which the student interacts with the instructor and other students. . . . Laptop use discourages students from this kind of participation."[2] Teachers who agree with Thagard usually do not allow cell phones or other electronic devices in their classrooms, believing instead that the classroom interaction between teacher and students is of the utmost importance and that electronic devices are a distraction from this interaction.

Other educators, such as Gord Taylor of Craik School in Saskatchewan, Canada, take the opposite view. Taylor says, "We would be burying our heads in the sand if we said that cell phones were not a part of everyday life. I don't know a businessman out there who doesn't carry a cell phone. I don't know a lawyer or accountant out there who doesn't carry a cell phone. Why wouldn't we have them in schools?"[3] Taylor's school is piloting a program where eighth- and ninth-grade classrooms are using cell phones as a regular part of their curriculum. Educators that agree with him believe that since a significant number of students have

Due to teens' increasing use of portable electronic devices, educators are being challenged to determine whether the devices should play a role in the classroom.

cell phones, it is better to turn them into a useful tool instead of condemning them as a distraction.

As cell phones, tablet computers, netbooks, and other portable devices become more and more prevalent in the lives of young people, educators will continue to face the question of whether or not to allow these devices in the classroom and, if they are allowed, how to use them to maximize their positive effects on students' learning.

Issues That Concern You: Electronic Devices in Schools presents a variety of viewpoints addressing the issue of the role of electronic devices in classrooms and in students' lives. Some focus on general aspects of whether electronic devices should be allowed in schools. Others consider whether schools should provide devices or whether students should use their own. Several of the viewpoints focus specifically on the use of cell phones in schools, including ways in which text messaging can be a distraction or a support for learning. In addition, this volume contains several appendixes to help the reader understand and explore the topic, including a bibliography and a list of organizations to contact for further information. The appendix titled "What You Should Know About Electronic Devices in Schools" offers facts and survey results about cell phones, laptops, and other devices. The appendix "What You Should Do About Electronic Devices in Schools" offers suggestions on becoming better informed about the use of technology in classrooms and ways to advocate for change. With all these features, *Issues That Concern You: Electronic Devices in Schools* provides a thorough resource for readers interested in this timely issue.

Notes

1. Quoted in Sharon Shinn, "Dial M for Mobile," *Biz Ed*, January/February 2009.
2. Paul Thagard, "Banning Laptops in Classrooms," *Hot Thought* (blog), PsychologyToday.com, July 9, 2010. www.psychology today.com/blog/hot-thought/201007/banning-laptops-in-class rooms-0.
3. Quoted in David Rapp, "Lift the Cell Phone Ban," Scholastic Administrator, n.d. www.scholastic.com/browse/article.jsp ?id=3751073.

ONE

Electronic Devices Can Be Useful Learning Tools

Day Rosenberg

> Day Rosenberg is director of the upper school at Far Hills Country Day School in Far Hills, New Jersey. In this viewpoint, Rosenberg compares cell phones and other electronic devices with communication innovations of the past. He asserts that people's attitudes toward innovations have been wary for centuries—when the alphabet was invented Plato worried that memorization skills would decline and people would have less quality time together. Rosenberg points out a number of positive educational uses for technology and recommends that educators make use of them instead of worrying about potential problems.

Yo-Yos, Pokémon trading cards, Rubik's Cubes, Wacky Wall Walkers, and Whoopee Cushions are some of the classic contraband that have made their way into classrooms over the years—and into the drawers at the bottom of teachers' desks. The students' desire to show-and-tell the latest fad in gadgetry is ever present in our schools. Today, the novelty items undoubtedly require batteries and flow out of the cornucopia of electronica du jour, my personal favorite being the silver-dollar-sized electronic virtual pet, which needs to be fed and exercised, or else it will end up in the virtual pet cemetery.

The current generation of popular student electronica includes cell phones, iPods, and the language of text messaging. Unlike the electronica of years past, they pose a more difficult question for educators. Do we cast the latest incarnation of electronic novelty into the teacher drawer half-filled with silly string and chattering teeth and the like, or do we contextualize these powerful new communication tools into the category of notebooks, calculators, and pencil boxes? In other words, are they simply highly sophisticated tools of goofing around, or can they be serious tools of learning? My view is that, as educators, we need a fair and balanced approach to the potential application of today's "it" gadgetry, corroborated with a vibrant, community-enhancing honor code and advisory system.

Technology Has Improved Student Writing Skills

Al Filreis, director of the Center for Programs in Contemporary Writing at the University of Pennsylvania, deals with high school writers as well as college students. In the past 20 years, he told a *Christian Science Monitor* reporter, he has seen "the quality of student writing at the high school level [go] way up, and this is explained by the fact that they do more writing than they ever did." Overall, says Filreis, whatever the societal worries about teens morphing into fleet-fingered, e-mail-happy robots, there's a genuine writing renaissance under way. "We lost it in the 1950s and 1960s," he says, when telephones and TVs poured into American homes and daily writing dwindled to grocery lists and office memos. "I think we've gained it back. After a period of normal writing went away, the Internet revolution brought back writing in the daily sense."

People have been concerned about the adverse effects of new communication tools ever since Plato worried that the alphabet would cause us to lose our memorization skills and cut down on our quality time together, says Howard Rheingold, a longtime technology watcher and author of *Smart Mobs: The Next Social Revolution*. Regardless of where teens text, debating whether they should use the new technology "is somewhat futile," Rheingold says. "They're going to do it." And, he adds, adults probably will continue to adopt texting as well as other new forms of communication. Why? It fulfills a deep need. "We've had speech," Rheingold says. "We've had writing. We've had the alphabet. We've had the printing press. These are technologies for extending the way we think and communicate. That's what humans do: We come up with new ways to communicate and new ways to build civilizations." Is that a mindless rock song being listened to on the iPod, or is the student memorizing his lines for the musical, or listening to the latest lecture made available by U.C. Berkeley?

Ten years ago, we were discussing whether or not we should embrace the Internet as an academic tool; time has yielded us an obvious answer—and lesson. Yes, challenges exist with MySpace and YouTube, but the real problem is that it's hard to be open to the idea of embracing such technology when most of what we hear is the negative. The amazing projects, documentaries, and music and language lessons don't get quite the same quiver out of a sensation-driven media. Yet, these positives are significant—and becoming clearer to educators every day. We are now weaving the Internet into our curriculum with greater sophistication and greater results.

Educators Should Use the Power of Technology

But what are we to make of these new devices—these palm-sized computers and cell phones that reek of cutting-edge technology? Isn't this going too far? Shouldn't we worry that they offer more distraction than benefit? Aren't they undermining our efforts at teaching, as evidenced by students who photograph tests and send them to friends on their buddy lists?

Technology expert Marc Prensky joins me in cajoling administrators to reconsider their view of using mobile phone technology—not to fear the worst, but to imagine a more global approach that embraces the educational potential of such technology. Yes, students will occasionally use hand-held devices for mindless stuff—and, on rare occasions, to cheat (although the latter, I believe, can be effectively addressed). But cell phones, essentially

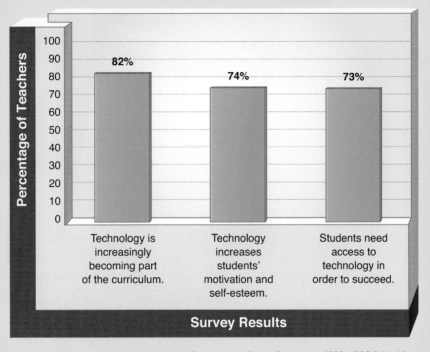

Teachers Weigh in on Technology and Education

Percentage of Teachers

82% — Technology is increasingly becoming part of the curriculum.

74% — Technology increases students' motivation and self-esteem.

73% — Students need access to technology in order to succeed.

Survey Results

Taken from: Survey conducted by the International Psychoanalytic Studies Organization (IPSO), IPSO Public Affairs, February 23–March 2, 2011.

micro-computers, also have great academic value. For instance, they can support language lessons, display animations of medical and chemical processes, be used for polling and testing, and serve as the gateway to larger learning resources. Prensky also explains to educators that, in a flattened world, while American educators are busy banning cell phones in schools in an effort to control what they barely understand, students in China, Japan, the Philippines, and Germany are using their mobile phones to learn English, to study math and spelling, and to access university lectures. Prensky reminds us that the average cell phone has more computing power than many of the computers of 10 years ago. Then he asks the all-important question: "How can we harness that power in education?"

A cell phone dictionary application, or app, is seen here. Some educators believe that many apps can be useful learning tools.

Cell-Phone Applications Can Be Educational

Between Samsung and the Apple store, there are over 150 educational applications available for purchase and download, and there are hundreds more free on the Internet. Some of my favorite cell-phone educational applications:

Rocketron—It enables you to get the latest news by categories like sports, politics, music.

Textnovel—It enables you to create your own public or private novel. You don't have to wait to work on your writing until you are home in front of the computer. Textnovel can also be used as an on-the-go-research notebook. Have you heard about the Japanese writer who texted her entire bestseller?

Foneshow—This is a wonderful mobile resource for downloading podcasts, or for creating your own. There are excellent podcasts on just about every subject. Students can also easily generate their own podcast radioshows.

Earfl—With Earfl, when you speak through your cell phone, your messages are transcribed and e-mailed to you or any of your contacts. These messages can then be sent to different e-mail addresses. (A similar product is Jott.)

Kwiry—Text 59479 and a subject of interest and Kwiry will run a complete web search and then e-mail the search results to several e-mail addresses. This is a particularly powerful research tool that can be very helpful when students are doing group projects.

ChaCha—This is an electronic version of the reference librarian. You call with a researchable question, and it texts back the answer.

Polleverywhere—In a nation obsessed with polling, this program easily generates polls where voters can text their opinions.

Museum411—A wonderful tool for self-guided and self-paced listening tours of museums.

CNN iReporter—Students can record and send news stories to CNN, and later visit at CNN's iReporter space. Designate a reporter on your next field trip. Using a videophone, the reporter can record, upload, and then share his or her personal newscast.

All of these applications are in use by teachers nationwide—and they all have accompanying websites that make joining both simple and streamlined. Care to do a technology magic trick with your students? In front of the class, have them ask you a factoid—say, "What is the population of Canada?" By texting 46645 (GOOGL), you will have an answer in about 20 seconds. Trust me, you will have your students' attention.

Worry about micro-technology being a distraction or problem in schools is overblown. Honor codes, technology agreements, "do the right thing" messages, and classic character education delivered through an empowered advisory program can develop a student's integrity to deal with ever-changing electronic gadgetry. I wouldn't count on hyperscrutinized student handbooks, where students are sent searching for the omnipresent loophole, to do this work for us. We need to actively teach students right from wrong—regardless of technology, but perhaps more carefully because of the power of technology. Will we prevent all problems? No. But blaming the technology is not the answer. If a terribly mean-spirited, student-composed note were intercepted by a savvy teacher, you wouldn't ban the pen, would you?

TWO

More Schools Are Encouraging the Use of Electronic Devices

Ian Quillen

Ian Quillen is a journalist who writes about educational issues. In this viewpoint, Quillen considers several schools that have begun encouraging students to bring their own mobile devices, especially smartphones, to school for use in the classroom. He points out that it is more affordable for schools to provide the remaining students with devices to borrow, rather than trying to equip all students with laptops. Quillen considers some of the potential misuses, such as texting in class, and concludes that students need to learn to use their devices appropriately, the same way they will when they become adults in the business world.

At Oak Hills High School in suburban Cincinnati, students returned from summer break [in 2010] to learn they were free not only to bring their mobile devices to school, but also to use them—at their teachers discretion—to connect to the school's wireless network to do their work.

At Cumberland Valley High near Harrisburg, Pa., district officials have approved a similar policy on a pilot basis after deep and repeated discussions with administrators, teachers, and parents.

Ian Quillen, "Schools Open Doors to Students' Mobile Devices," *Digital Directions,* vol. 4, no. 1, October 20, 2010, pp. 30–35. Copyright © Editorial Projects in Education, Inc. All rights reserved. Reproduced by permission.

And in Chicago, the Mikva Challenge student-leadership branch suggested in an August report that the city's public schools allow students to use their own smartphones on campus for learning.

"The students do see [a smartphone] as a potential learning tool," says Jessica Gingold, an education-council program coordinator for the Mikva Challenge, a nonprofit group dedicated

Fourth graders use iPads to study Spanish. Many schools are encouraging students to bring their own cell phones, tablets, and other mobile devices to school.

to developing young civic leaders, activists, and policymakers by exposing them to political opportunities. "But that's not their [primary message]. Their [message] is that we need to start changing the policy, and using the resources that are already available."

The point, say proponents of mobile learning, is not that discussions about enabling such learning are at varying stages, but that they are happening at all. More educators are wising up, they say, to the reality that most students have phones or other mobile devices that could allow them to give real-time feedback to a lecture on a text-message back channel, take pictures during a science field trip, or answer teacher prompts with online polling.

And with the increasing capabilities and prevalence of mobile devices, the growing demand for K–12 students to be comfortable learning online, and the shrinking technology budgets of districts coping with the aftermath of the Great Recession, allowing students to use their own mobile devices is making more sense to more people.

"I think it's a discussion that is taking place in almost every school district," says Todd Yohey, the superintendent of Ohio's 8,100-student Oak Hills school district, which includes Oak Hills High. "I think that for districts . . . with the resources to implement some programs, that it's probably already happening."

But superintendents and technology directors must consider what students are learning about technology use when they reshape mobile-device policies, ed-tech experts say. They must reach out to teachers and parents to explain how those policies forward students' learning. And, most importantly, they must revise their thinking about resources to conceive of school-owned hardware and student-owned hardware as one fleet.

Cellphones Are Less Expensive than Laptops

Recent research shows the proportion of students owning cellphones is increasing. A January [2010] survey from the Kaiser Family Foundation found about two-thirds of 8- to 18-year-olds owned cellphones, while more than three-quarters had an iPod or other MP3 media player. And an April study by the Pew Research Center's Internet & American Life Project reported that when you change the age bracket to 12- to 17-year-olds, 75 percent of students have cellphones—and often smartphones that are capable of completing many of the same online functions as laptop computers and netbooks.

Yohey says the expectation at Oak Hills has never been that every student would someday own a cellphone—only that enough would so that the district could supply devices to those who didn't. It's a strategy other districts making similar policy shifts are following in pursuit of a 1-to-1 computing environment in which every student has his or her own digital-learning device.

"The cost of having some cellphones you can provide, at least in school during school time, is small compared to supplying laptops or supplying broadband in people's homes," says Christopher Dede, a professor of educational technology at the Harvard Graduate School of Education.

For Oak Hills, Yohey said it cost the district $236,000 to wire the high school's filtered Internet network for wireless service throughout the building. Loaner mobile devices for students cost about $500, and would not need a data plan to connect to the school's open network. Netbooks would have a cost similar to mobile phones, but would have to be distributed to a greater portion of the student body.

Districts that can't afford to wire entire schools can still pick strategic hot spots, says Robert Scidmore, the director of technology for the 10,700-student Eau Claire Area district in western Wisconsin. That's the plan for his district, where officials are putting the finishing touches on a new cellphone policy that would allow students to use the phones at their leisure between classes, and teachers to dictate how they were used during class.

"By the end of the year, we hope to have hot spots at both district high schools," says Scidmore. "Libraries, study halls, auditoriums, gymnasiums—we want to at least get those wired."

And while most technology directors agree that, ideally, students without mobile devices would be provided loaners from

Cell Phone Ownership

Cell phone use by children and teens is growing rapidly.

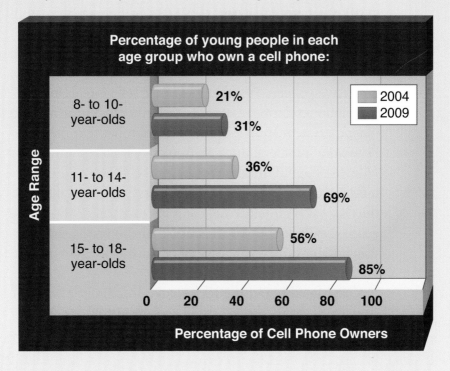

Percentage of young people in each age group who own a cell phone:

- 8- to 10-year-olds: 21% (2004), 31% (2009)
- 11- to 14-year-olds: 36% (2004), 69% (2009)
- 15- to 18-year-olds: 56% (2004), 85% (2009)

Age Range — Percentage of Cell Phone Owners

Taken from: Victoria J. Rideout et al. *Generation M²: Media in the Lives of 8– 18-Year-Olds; A Kaiser Family Foundation Study*. Menlo Park, CA: Henry J. Kaiser Family Foundation, 2010. www.kff.org/entmedia/upload/8010.pdf.

their districts, there are still ways to explore using only student-owned devices.

For example, says Juli Di Chiro, the superintendent of the 3,000-student Ashland district in southwestern Oregon, teachers could make the very simple request of asking cellphone owners to pair up with non-owners for an assignment.

"Even at two-to-one, that's a lot better than what we [actually] do right now" in the district, says Di Chiro, who, for now, is only informally considering changing the district's cellphone policy. "Even if we have 50 percent of the kids [owning devices], . . . the ubiquitousness [pervasiveness] of this technology is just going to be increasing as we move forward."

Abuse of Cellphones During Class Is a Behavioral Issue

But recognizing the dramatically increased presence and potential of student-owned cellphones is only one step toward enacting less restrictive policies. Another, Scidmore says, is realizing that abuse of cellphones during class time—whether for cheating, accessing inappropriate material, or sending improper text messages—is a behavioral problem, not a technology problem.

In his Eau Claire district, the new policy awaiting passage reflects that perspective. Not only does it enable teachers to have the final say on in-class use, but it also enables them through language that is only three sentences long, implying that any other issues not covered explicitly fall under the district's general code of conduct.

Kyle Menchhofer, the technology coordinator for the 2,200-student St. Mary's city school system in Ohio, contends that besides allowing for academic use, a successful cellphone policy should help educate students about proper conduct with a device that is nearly universal in the work world. Currently, his district uses federal economic-stimulus funds to help provide students in grades 3–6 with district-issued smartphones and does not allow students to use their own devices. But a change to that policy, he says, is something he would support.

"What we need to do as schools is to teach our kids to be responsible users," Menchhofer says. "There's an appropriate time to use the device and not use the device. If I'm teaching and lecturing, you should not have that device out. If you get it out while I'm teaching or lecturing, you're going to lose your privacy and have to go back to pencil and paper."

The St. Mary's district also makes sure its students use only the devices' Internet features, by disabling phone and text-message functions—in part, Menchhofer says, to gain parents' trust that students won't abuse the phones.

Parents and Teachers Need to Be Educated

In districts that are revising their cellphone-use policies, gaining that trust appears to be a crucial step.

Lenny Schad, the chief information officer for the 59,000-student Katy Independent School District in Houston's western suburbs, is hoping that a pilot program that will begin allowing elementary students at one school to use their own devices this winter will expand through the district the following year. He says he hopes to have public support for the project, in part, because other district parents have already experienced a continuing initiative in which 1,500 students at 10 elementary campuses are using district-issued smartphones.

"The biggest thing school districts have to do is to prepare the community for this," Schad says. "You have to spend time working with parents, answering questions and concerns, and helping them understand why we're doing something like this."

In Pennsylvania's 7,700-student Cumberland Valley district, situated a few miles west of Harrisburg, school officials say they held discussions with teachers, staff members, parents, and other community members for nearly all of the 2009–10 school year before deciding to allow students to use their own devices this fall. The discussions developed not only out of a desire to explore new learning methods, but also to address chronic cellphone-related discipline issues.

"Some of them kind of got a little heated," says Darren DiCello, a district instructional technology specialist. "There were teachers who felt like it was almost a control issue, because they wanted to be able to tell the kids they weren't able to have the phone. . . . People had their thoughts either way, but I think most of the teachers that sat on that committee wanted something to be done so there would be consistency across the building."

The pilot program ends at the end of the first academic quarter, but if feedback is favorable, it can be extended until the standard policy is changed. Cumberland Valley district officials say reviews from faculty and staff members were mixed in the first two weeks of the academic year.

Trial and Error Will Produce the Best Advances

Dede of the Harvard Graduate School of Education stresses that, while an eventual progression to open mobile-learning environments might be inevitable, that doesn't mean it will be immediately beneficial. The learning potential of the devices, he says, won't be realized without continuing professional development, as well as in-class trial and error.

"The enthusiasts in the technology community treat each new development as magic," Dede says, "even though we have generation after generation after generation of proof that there is no such thing as magic."

But he acknowledges differences between other movements and the mobile-learning movement. For one, he says, while previous education technologies have developed first in postsecondary education and trickled down into K–12, some mobile-learning applications are already popular among parents of prekindergartners.

That could mean a "bidirectional" push of mobile learning into education's mainstream, he says, which could help parents become comfortable with mobile learning in school even if they weren't with similar initiatives using laptops, for example.

Elliot Soloway, an electrical-engineering and computer-science professor at the University of Michigan, in Ann Arbor, and the founder of the Center for Highly Interactive Computing in Education, insists the differences go a bit further. The ability to access the Internet through a device whose cost is a fraction of that of a laptop, he says, potentially gives students rich and poor the "unprecedented" ability to answer their own questions. Moreover, he argues, trusting a student to use a cellphone properly creates more-responsible students.

But, while some districts have rehashed policies to explore that potential, most have not. As Dede puts it, there are still considerable (and understandable) reservations about putting teachers in positions where they could become entangled, for instance, in a case of in-class sexting or cheating.

Thinking of Cellphones as Educational Tools

And students who haven't been exposed to the possibility of using cellphones for learning rarely push for that opportunity themselves, because restrictive school policies have made the idea seem out of the question, experts say.

The experience of the 15 high school students on Chicago's Mikva Challenge education council supports that argument. When asked by Chicago schools chief Ron Huberman to draw up a report suggesting improvements to the 409,000-student district's technology profile, students said they first envisioned school-issued laptops and free Wi-Fi networks. It wasn't until meeting with a teacher who explained the possibilities of mobile learning that they included that suggestion in their report.

"She was the first teacher to actually come and tell us how she used" the phone for educational purposes, says Lisa Jean Baptiste, a junior at Harper High School. "Students wouldn't think they can use their cellphones educationally because they haven't been told they can use them educationally."

iPods Can Help Students Learn

Kathleen Kennedy Manzo

In this viewpoint, *Education Week* journalist Kathleen Kennedy Manzo discusses the iPod as a tool for learning. Manzo's focus is on Georgia, where grant money has been used to fund an initiative in sixty high schools across the state to provide hand-held technology to students. She highlights some of the uses of iPods in classrooms at Roswell High School in suburban Atlanta—including accessing podcasts and notes from class lectures as well as related video clips. Manzo also discusses several other schools across the country that have initiated similar projects.

Students can use their iPod touches in plain sight in Mark Schuler's World History class at Roswell High School here [in Roswell, Georgia]. The portable devices and the telltale ear buds are also welcome in the hallways, library, and cafeteria.

Roswell officials, unlike most of their counterparts around the country, have changed their view of the MP3 players, seeing them less as contraband and more as educational accessories. Educators at the 2,400-student school in suburban Atlanta are hoping to put more content at students' fingertips and capture their interest by

Kathleen Kennedy Manzo, "Educators Embrace iPods for Learning," *Education Week*, vol. 29, no. 26, pp. 16–17. Copyright © 2010 by Editorial Projects in Education, Inc. All rights reserved. Reproduced by permission.

enlisting the digital tools today's teenagers have already mastered for social and leisure purposes.

"Five years ago iPods were banned, but we got overwhelmed with trying to discipline kids and fight the technology," says Edward Spurka, the principal of Roswell High. "Our philosophy here now is let them have it, . . . so we've allowed all those resources out in the world to be on their person."

The school's pilot program, which integrates iPods into Advanced Placement (AP) classes and encourages appropriate applications for other lessons and activities across the curriculum, was introduced as part of Georgia's educational technology plan. The initiative, being rolled out in 60 high schools across the state, uses federal funding for hand-held technologies as a means of

A teacher's drawer holds confiscated cell phones and iPods. Some schools, however, now allow students to use their electronic devices in the classroom as educational tools.

expanding access to and success in rigorous high school courses for underrepresented student groups.

"We thought this would be a great way to engage learners and deliver more-rigorous material to them," says Becky Chambers, who manages the AP program for the Georgia Department of Education. "Oftentimes, kids have technology but they don't use it for substantive work, only social media or for pleasure such as listening to music. They don't recognize the power of these devices to improve knowledge and skills."

The state program provides grants of up to $64,000 to districts—funded primarily from federal Enhancing Education Through Technology, or EETT, grants—to buy the portable devices and provide professional development and support services to teachers in AP courses.

Several Schools Are Using iPods

The touch-screen devices—which are equipped with wireless Internet capability, play high-quality video, and can be equipped with any of thousands of free educational applications, or apps— have found favor in a number of schools across the country. First graders in Orange County, Calif., for example, are using iPods to record themselves reading aloud and retelling a story in their own words to demonstrate comprehension. In Springfield, Ill., teachers can create podcasts, or audio recordings, of lessons and provide links to related online resources that students can access at any time using their hand-held computers. And 3rd graders in Wells, Maine, are using iPods to preview exhibits at the Ogunquit Museum of American Art as they prepare their own podcasts related to a field trip.

At Roswell High, Schuler's students have round-the-clock access to the class Web site, where there are links to text resources, podcasts and notes from previous lectures, video clips on related topics, and details about assignments and exams. The students often take notes or compose drafts of essays on the miniature keypads using word-processing software and then send them to themselves via e-mail. Schuler gives multiple-choice quizzes on

Teen Gadget Ownership, 2008–2009

Percentage of teens aged 12–17 who own each gadget:

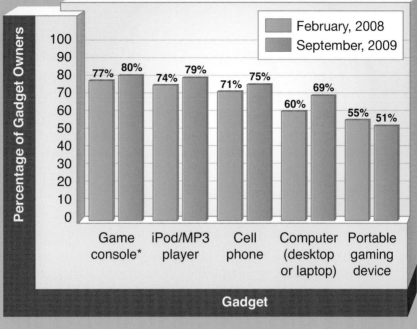

*Not a significant change between years.

Taken from: Amanda Lenhart et al. "Teens and Mobile Phones," Pew Internet & American Life Project, April 20, 2010.

the devices, which then automatically calculate scores and provide data on students' knowledge of the content.

"With the [iPod] touches, I'm not bound to the 55 minutes of class time," he says. "They have expanded my time with students, and if they are willing to put in the work, they can learn at their own pace and easily find more information on their own."

When he sees students hunched over their iPods typing furiously, Schuler sometimes wonders if they are attending to classwork or something unrelated. Ultimately, he's learned to trust they will do the necessary work, generally a given among his high-achieving students, he says.

iPods Have Advantages over Smartphones

The experiment at Roswell is still limited to two classrooms—Schuler's as well as an English literature class—where students are issued iPods. But other teachers are finding ways to do similar activities using students' personal devices. Spurka and other administrators use their own iPods to document classroom observations and collect data on teachers' performance.

The iPod touches are appealing for educators and students alike because of their ease of use, the availability of free educational applications, and ready Internet access, according to Lisa Thumann, a senior specialist in technology education at Rutgers University's Busch Campus in Piscataway, N.J., where she teaches a class for educators who want to use the devices as teaching or administrative tools.

In Thumann's view, cellphones or smartphones offer more instructional options for teachers than MP3 players, because large numbers of middle and high school students have their own, and applications are adaptable across brands and types. While many students own MP3 players, it would be harder to coordinate lessons when some students have Apple's iPods while others have Sony's Walkman or Dell's Zune devices, Thumann says.

But the iPods and similar devices don't require costly data plans and, without telephone and texting capabilities or camera features, they tend to alleviate some of the concerns over cybersafety and inappropriate use that have made many school administrators prohibit cellphones in schools, according to Kathy Politis, the director of technology for the Fulton County school district, which includes Roswell High.

For officials in Georgia, the MP3 players provide the ideal solution for using mobile technology efficiently and effectively in schools.

"We've been struggling to move teacher instruction away from some of the more traditional approaches to formats that are more engaging for students," says Elizabeth Webb, the state's director of innovative academic programs. "We're giving them a great tool not only for them to be successful in high school, but when they get out in the real world."

iPads Could Hinder Teaching, Professors Say

Ben Wieder

In this viewpoint, journalist Ben Wieder discusses the usefulness of iPads and other tablet devices in the classroom. Wieder notes some advantages to iPads, including their portability, long battery life, and appeal for students. Some educators, however, report that the iPad has a limited usefulness—its touchscreen keypad does not work well for taking notes, and a good stylus to be used for handwriting has not been developed yet. Other tablets offer more interactivity, but they have drawbacks, too. Wieder suggests that in the end what students themselves want to use dictates which devices schools and colleges adopt.

Rival tablet PC's foster more interactivity, studies suggest. But students' craving for the Apple devices could matter more.

When Paul Steinhaus, chief information officer at Chatham University, met with his colleagues last summer to discuss getting iPads for incoming students, they knew the move could raise the profile of the small institution in Pittsburgh. Across the country, institutions had grabbed headlines for adopting Apple's tablet computing device.

Ben Wieder, "iPads Could Hinder Teaching, Professors Say," *Chronicle of Higher Education*, vol. 57, no. 28, pp. A22–A23. Copyright © 2010 by the Chronicle of Higher Education. All rights reserved. Reproduced by permission.

But Mr. Steinhaus and other administrators soon realized that the iPad, with the slow finger-typing it requires, actually makes written course work more difficult, and that the devices wouldn't run all of the university's applications. "I'd hate to charge students and have them only be able to use it for e-mail and Facebook," says Mr. Steinhaus. Chatham charges a $700 annual technology fee, which now pays for standard laptops.

Still, he adds wistfully, "it would have been nice to get the publicity out of it."

Despite the iPad's popularity—Apple has sold nearly 15 million of them and just came out with the iPad2; and there are dozens of competitors, like the Samsung Galaxy—early studies indicate that these finger-based tablets are passive devices that have limited use in higher education. They are great for viewing media and allow students to share readings. But professors cannot use them to mark up material on the fly and show changes to students in response to their questions, a type of interactivity that has been a major thrust in pedagogy.

Even students have issues. When the University of Notre Dame tested iPads in a management class, students said the finger-based interface on its glassy surface was not good for taking class notes and didn't allow them to mark up readings. For their online final exam, 39 of the 40 students put away their iPads in favor of a laptop, because of concerns that the Apple tablet might not save their material.

"When they're working on something important, it kind of freaks them out," says Corey M. Angst, the assistant professor of management who tested the tablets.

For some professors, an older, less-hyped model of tablet computer offers far more advantages. That device is the tablet PC. It's clunkier than the iPad—and so uncool that it runs Windows—but it allows instructors and students to write precisely because it uses a penlike stylus, and to type quickly on its attached keyboard.

Pluses and Minuses

Keyboardless, finger-based tablets like the iPad do have several advantages over laptops and tablet PC's. Their smaller size and

A teacher prepares student lessons on an iPad. Though good for viewing materials, the devices, many teachers say, are too limited in interactivity for most classwork.

extended battery life means that students can, and do, carry them around without having to worry about finding a wall outlet.

Mr. Angst could send articles to students hours before classes met with the confidence that they would receive the articles on their iPads and be prepared to discuss them.

At Reed College, having all the texts available in a political-science class on the iPad meant it was easier to refer to readings and pull in outside material for discussion, says Martin Ringle, the college's chief technology officer.

iPads also foster collaboration. Students using them for group assignments in a math class at Pepperdine University were more in sync than were students in a section not using iPads. The iPad-equipped students worked at the same pace as one another and shared their screens to help one another solve tough problems, says Dana Hoover, assistant chief information officer for communications and planning.

Laptop screens can create a barrier to discussion—and also hide unrelated Web browsing—and Ms. Hoover says students were more engaged in classes using the iPad because those barriers were removed.

But these iPad pluses are countered by a fair number of drawbacks.

Annotating texts is a big one. Course readings were converted to PDF's at Reed, which allowed students to mark them up using an application called iAnnotate, but Mr. Ringle acknowledges that this wouldn't work for all classes, because many texts can't easily be converted to PDF's, and many electronic textbooks don't allow annotation.

Instructors also worry that, at least for now, fewer textbooks are available for the iPad, which requires special formatting. For instance, Mr. Angst's Notre Dame class used a textbook from the e-textbook vendor CourseSmart, but found that it had limited options for annotation.

That may improve soon. The academic publisher McGraw-Hill is working with a software company called Inkling, which makes textbooks iPad-friendly with multimedia-rich text that allows note-taking. "It goes well beyond a reading experience; it's more of an interactive experience," says Vineet Madan, vice president for learning ecosystems at McGraw-Hill.

But only nine of the company's 1,500 higher-education titles are currently available through Inkling, although Mr. Madan says the total should reach 100 of the most popular titles by next year.

Other content providers are taking a wait-and-see approach to iPads and other slates.

DyKnow, an educational-software company, makes a program that is often paired with tablet PC's. Functioning as a virtual, interactive whiteboard, it allows professors to mark up lecture material, share it with students, and accept and display in-class work from them, the company says. Mr. Steinhaus, who championed use of DyKnow at Chatham, says it made classes, particularly in the math and the sciences, more visual and interactive.

Michael Vasey, sales manager at DyKnow, says it is tracking new tablets but is hesitant to start adapting its Windows-based program to the newer formats.

"We're waiting for that killer device to come out," he says. "If there was a clear leader that was doing this, it would make it more compelling." He would like to see a device with both pen and finger-touch capabilities.

The Lure of Tablet PC's

Actually, such a machine already exists. Beth Simon, a lecturer in the computer-science department at the University of California at San Diego, owns a tablet PC made by Lenovo that has both finger and pen-based sensors.

It wasn't the answer for her. She says she stopped using the finger option because it was impossible to write. "My finger wasn't pointy enough," she says.

As an instructor, Ms. Simon relies on writing with tablet PC's to foster interactivity. She helped develop Ubiquitous Presenter, a free program similar to DyKnow. It works particularly well in large lecture classes, she says, because it brings the professor's notes to each student, and the submission of in-class assignments makes diagnoses easier when students have trouble with new concepts.

If professors can't write, that interaction is impossible, she says.

Stylus inputs are available for the iPad, but William G. Griswold, a computer-science professor at San Diego, says they don't solve the problem.

When people write with a pen, they frequently rest their hand on the page to give them more control, he explains. The iPad and other finger-based devices would detect the resting hand as well as the stylus, throwing off the input process. (Mr. Griswold and Ms. Simon have received support from PC makers to test their tablets.)

Apple seems to be aware of the issue. The *New York Times*'s Bits blog has reported that Apple filed a patent for a stylus with a built-in accelerometer that relies on motion, rather than the screen's touch sensor, to determine what's being written. But Apple hasn't said when, if ever, the device would be available.

The extra precision afforded by a stylus is particularly important, Mr. Griswold says, because of the small size of the tablet screen—seven to 10 inches in diameter for the models released so far. Even larger models have screens two to three inches smaller than most tablet PC's.

While Apple has promoted the iPad's ability to change learning, Ms. Simon says that as far as she knows, the company isn't working with leaders in the learning process: professors themselves.

Apple didn't provide discounted hardware or extra support for any institution in this article, and the company says it has scaled back support of conferences and hardware donations.

It's not just Apple. Robert H. Reed, a marketing consultant who worked at both Microsoft and Hewlett-Packard promoting tablet PC's to colleges, thinks computer makers have been less focused on higher education during the recent economic downturn.

In the 1990s, Microsoft largely financed the development of a precursor to Ubiquitous Presenter at the University of Washington, and Hewlett-Packard donated equipment to the university for a tablet PC lab and sponsored academic conferences. Nothing like that is happening now, even though HP is about to bring out its own iPad competitor, the TouchPad.

Student Choice

Despite professors' preferences for other machines, the choice of education tools may belong not to them, but to their students.

"Jimmy! Will you stop texting on your mobile phone. We are trying to discuss how technology has changed society!"

"Jimmy! Will you stop texting on your mobile phone. We are trying to discuss how technology has changed society!" cartoon by Phil Judd. www.CartoonStock.com.

Tablet PC's have never caught on with the consumer market, and Ms. Simon, at San Diego, says most of her students have never even heard of them. They are priced high, and even their partisans admit they are not easy to use.

The iPad, in contrast, is intuitive to use and relatively inexpensive, says Reed's Mr. Ringle. That's a powerful draw. At the conclusion of its study, Reed offered participating students the option of purchasing iPads at a $250 discount, half off the $499 base model. All of them did.

As competition from multiple manufacturers drives down the prices of newer tablets, Mr. Ringle thinks more students will be likely to bring them to campus.

Some of the devices may prove more conducive to education than others, but consumer decisions rather than educational ones will probably determine which tablets students purchase—and which ones colleges will support, he says.

"I don't think the institution is going to get to decide about the uptake of these devices," Mr. Ringle says. Colleges, and their professors, will have to adapt to their students' choice whether they like it or not. That hasn't happened yet, but as more content becomes available, he is confident it will.

FIVE

Bring-Your-Own-Laptop Programs Help Education

Jeff Weinstock

In this viewpoint, journalist Jeff Weinstock discusses school programs in which students are encouraged to bring their own laptops or other devices to school. He explains that many school districts that began providing laptops for every student could not afford to continue this practice and that having students bring their own laptops is the next best thing. He discusses some of the challenges of this type of program, which include setting up security to prevent students from hacking into the school's computer system, preparing guidelines, choosing software that can be used on a variety of devices, and providing devices for students who cannot afford them.

With cost concerns squeezing districts out of 1-to-1 computing programs, a once unthinkable solution is now in play: allowing students to bring their own laptops, PDAs, and—heaven help us—cell phones.

At Empire High School in Vail, AZ, every student has a laptop, a fully loaded MacBook supplied free of charge—to the student, at least—courtesy of the Vail School District. "We provide the entire experience," says Vail CIO [chief information officer] Matt Federoff.

Jeff Weinstock, "Left to Their Own Devices," *THE Journal*, vol. 37, no. 1, January 2010, pp. 32–36.

The 1-to-1 program is a cornerstone of Vail's Beyond Textbooks initiative, whose goal is an all-digital curriculum. So facing the decision on whether to expand the program to another of its high schools, Cienega, the district made the obvious choice: No way.

"At 900 bucks a pop, we can't provide a laptop to every kid at every one of our high schools," Federoff says. "Economically, that's not sustainable for us. We can do it for 850 kids at Empire. We can't do it for 2,000 kids at Cienega."

But the district was in no mood to dial back on its push toward digital content, or widen the hallowed ratio of one computer per student. So Federoff and his group gathered to brainstorm alternatives. "We were thinking, 'What are some other models?'" Federoff says. "We have a high school that is 1-to-1 where we give you the widget. Well, what if you bring the widget? A lot of our kids have their own laptops. What if we leveraged these devices to see if they can be used for instruction? Is that better or worse, or somewhere in the middle? We chose a handful of classes and a few teachers just to see how it would pan out, if it was a practical solution."

In July [2009], Vail launched a bring-your-own-laptop program at Cienega High in about a dozen classes. The program, Federoff stresses, is still in its trial phase. "It's purely an experiment," he says. "Right now we're feeling our way through it." So far, feedback has been mixed, according to Federoff. Such niggling interferences as scheduling difficulties and getting the students to actually bring the devices to class have muddled the effort.

Better than Nothing

"I don't know if it's better, but the alternative would be nothing," Federoff says. "We wouldn't have a device at all. If nothing else, bring-your-own-laptop has enabled dozens and dozens of students access to technology in the classroom they otherwise wouldn't have."

It may be an imperfect approach—marked by labor-intensive infrastructural and logistical tasks—but allowing students to bring their own computing devices to class may be the inevitable solu-

Empire High School in Vail, Arizona, provides every student with a laptop. Some school districts have also been looking at bring-your-own-laptop programs to provide students access to online information while in class.

tion for districts that are under ever-constricting budgets but want to preserve a technology-enhanced education. It's not just student-owned laptops that schools are opening up to, but any web-enabled device, including PDAs, iPod Touches, and cell phones. Not too long ago this would have struck many educators as a deal with the devil, to invite such potential chaos into the classroom. But now it only seems sensible, or as Don Manderson, technology coordinator of Florida's Escambia County Schools, says simply, "just the right thing to do."

"We'd like to have the best student-to-computer ratio that we possibly can," says Manderson as his district aims for the launch of a student-owned-devices program later this school year. "We certainly can't afford 1-to-1. Our districtwide ratio is 3-to-1, 4-to-1, but we'd like to do better than that. When there are many devices out there owned by students that could help to fill that void of computers, and they're perfectly functional and they could be helping the instructional process, I don't know how much longer it'll be viable to say no."

Setting Up the System Is Complicated

Escambia is now near completing what is the central technical challenge of permitting the use of student-owned computing tools. It has taken the district two years to establish a guest "path" on

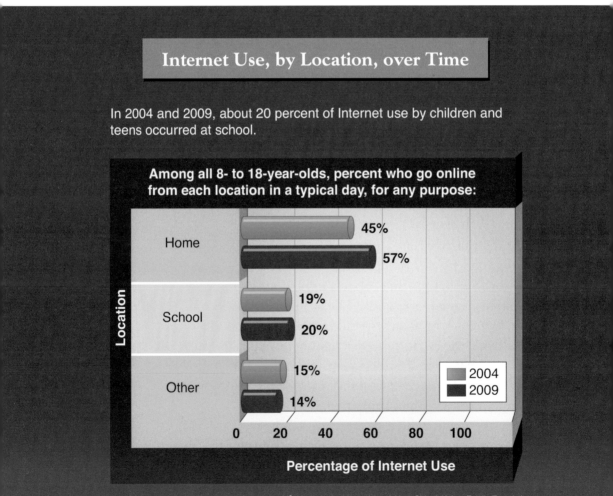

Internet Use, by Location, over Time

In 2004 and 2009, about 20 percent of Internet use by children and teens occurred at school.

Among all 8- to 18-year-olds, percent who go online from each location in a typical day, for any purpose:

Location

Home
- 45% (2004)
- 57% (2009)

School
- 19% (2004)
- 20% (2009)

Other
- 15% (2004)
- 14% (2009)

Percentage of Internet Use

0   20   40   60   80   100

2004
2009

Taken from: Victoria J. Rideout et al. *Generation M²: Media in the Lives of 8– 18-Year-Olds; A Kaiser Family Foundation Study*. Menlo Park, CA: Henry J. Kaiser Family Foundation, 2010. www.kff.org/entmedia/upload/8010.pdf.

the district network for student-owned devices that routes them through a web filter and on to the internet for study resources, but keeps them away from sensitive areas on the network meant only for staff and faculty.

"They can't get to our network operating system or mapped drives, or any other repositories of information that exist inside our firewall," Manderson says. "They go straight out the firewall, through the content filter, and out to the internet. That's all they can do."

The last component of the work has been the installation of FreeRADIUS, an open source RADIUS (remote authentication dial-in user service) server that will act as a gatekeeper to Escambia's secured network.

"We don't want a device that a student brings in with who-knows-what kind of hacking materials on it to be able to get to that network," he says. "Right now it would have access to the network because we don't have a login requirement. Until that is in place, we're postponing the rollout of the student appliances in the schools."

Acceptable Use Policies

Manderson says that installing the server has been done in tandem with another painstaking procedural step. It took the district two years to craft an addendum to its acceptable use policy (AUP) that lays out the parameters for the use of student-owned devices. "We've been very careful to define precisely what the limitations are and what the terms of use are," he says, "and what the terms of termination of the ability to use them are."

Manderson says this emphasis on identifying restrictions runs counter to the way acceptable use policies are now generally written. Two years ago he attended a conference session on drafting AUPs and learned that the trend was toward "defining expectations rather than defining what's not allowed." He says an orthodox approach suits the conservative community in which the district resides. "The policy may not be progressive, but the initiative is," he says.

The Escambia policy actually could be seen as a transgression of Florida state law, which Manderson says forbids cell phones from use in school except for emergency purposes. When is a cell phone not a cell phone? According to the Escambia AUP, when it's being used to get on the internet.

"The acceptable use policy treats the cell phone, if it's internet enabled, as an internet appliance," Manderson says. "If you're using it as an internet appliance and you're not using Skype or something like that to make a phone call, then I guess that would be acceptable use. But if you begin to use any cellular capabilities, including texting and instant messaging, then you would be in the area of inappropriate conduct."

Dealing with Different Devices

Crafting a policy to govern student-owned devices shows how troublesome it can be to bring so many disparate appliances under one standard. Things could get even thornier in the classroom, where a teacher may face a class of 30 students in which five have iPod Touches, five have laptops, five have PDAs, and five have old-school clamshell phones.

"If a teacher sends out a PDF study sheet, there may be kids with [appliances] that don't support PDFs as attachments," says Richard Doherty, co-founder and director of Envisioneering, a technology consulting group based in Seaford, NY. "Until issues like that are resolved, teachers and IT directors will be learning as they go, sending out two different formats of a file if necessary."

That scenario is also imagined by Karen Greenwood Henke, a Pasadena, CA–based ed tech consultant. "It would be frustrating for a teacher to find an amazing video on the internet that kids could see on their smartphones, but only half the students have phones that can play video," she says. "And of those, five need instruction on how to make their media player work."

So how can a consistent lesson be devised that allows every make and model of machine to participate? It's a top-of-mind concern for Vail's Federoff, who worries that the need to accommodate the capabilities of every device will force the teacher to simplify a lesson.

"The primary problem is, What does the teacher aim for?" he says, noting that this is one area where district-supplied machines have an advantage. "At Empire, if you provide the laptops, you know what applications [are installed], you know what the kids are capable of doing—you can ask everyone to make a movie. If the students bring the laptops, it gets trickier because you don't have a consistent tool set to aim for. My fear is you begin to go for the lowest common denominator: What do I know all the kids can do consistently? That actually isn't terribly exciting."

Software Must Be Available for All Devices

Vail's technology coordinator, Kevin Steeves, who also teaches ecology at Cienega High School, says Microsoft Excel, for example, isn't feasible because teachers have no assurance that every student will bring a laptop loaded with Excel. One application they can count on and therefore use liberally is the content management tool Moodle.

"That's a resource that no matter what laptop you have, you can access it," Steeves says. "The other thing we use a lot of is Google Apps. If teachers have a writing assignment, they'll focus on using Google Apps because they know all students have access to it."

One universal solution may have just entered North America six months ago. Norway-based ed tech provider It's Learning has just introduced to the US market a learning platform by the same name that can deliver educational materials for use on any web-enabled computing device, according to company president Jon Bower.

"It runs on the browser—it's not an app," he explains. "It runs beautifully on a Palm. It runs fine on a BlackBerry. It runs on an iPod. It runs on a PC, it runs on a Mac. It runs happily on an Xbox 360—in the browser. It is broadly device-independent, and it allows you to deliver content from just about any publisher."

The "real magic" of the platform, Bower believes, is its integration into a learning management system, which allows teachers to create their own learning materials that can then be delivered "seamlessly" with published third-party content to the students via their mobile devices. "That's how you get to really individualize the instruction process," he says.

Bower adds that It's Learning is well established abroad, used by more than 20 publishers to deliver their materials to European primary and higher education students. He says that in its short time in the US, the product is finding its target audience: "It's concentrated in schools that are highly focused on improving outcomes."

Schools Must Sometimes Provide Devices

Even if a cross-device platform makes its way into the classroom, that still doesn't resolve the question of what to do with those left out: the five kids in the class who have neither a Palm, an iPod Touch, a laptop, nor any web-enabled device whatsoever.

One answer is to keep spares on hand. Virginia's Hampton City Schools is currently conducting an experimental program at some of its middle schools in which students are creating videos with the use of their own video cameras. Any student who doesn't own a camera can check out one of the new video-enabled iPod Nanos the district has purchased. According to Director of Technology Georgianna Skinner, the district is hoping to have the same kind of store of reserve machines on hand when it implements a bring-your-own-devices initiative in the 2010–2011 school year.

The program comes on the heels of the termination of the district's 1-to-1 laptop plan, which Skinner says had to be scrapped because maintenance on the machines had become too pricey. "We had come to the point where we either had to refresh the laptops or we had to stop it," she says. "We had good results, but it was so expensive that we had to back off it. It was very disappointing."

Providing spares, though, for even just a portion of a 22,000-student-enrollment won't come all that cheap. "Surveys have told us that about 80 percent of our homes have internet access, so we're looking to fill in the 20 percent that don't," Skinner says. "What we're looking for is the least expensive device that will do what we need it to do."

Netbooks would seem to best fit that description; at around $400, they're cheaper than issuing textbooks to a student, which runs more toward $600 to $1,000 for four years of high school.

Vail's Federoff, however, thinks the device that will erase the digital divide is still out there. "Netbooks are close," he says. "There's some middle ground between an iPod Touch and a laptop. Somebody's going to create that device and that's going to be a transformative moment."

The "School-Bus Model"

Federoff ultimately sees a solution he compares to "a school-bus model," where the school offers a baseline machine but allows students to bring their own if they wish. "At some point we're going to provide a device that lets kids get to digital content, and it will have a consistent tool set and a consistent experience. We don't know what that device is; it hasn't been invented yet. What we'll say to the kids is, 'Okay, that's what you get.' If a kid's got a box that can do better, the kid can bring it. Kind of like, if you can drive yourself to school, you can—or you can ride the bus."

Until that day arrives, Manderson says that the availability of student-owned devices actually helps equalize the classroom experience for all by freeing up whatever amount of school-owned devices there are. "For every child who is able to bring a device to school, it makes another device available that the district provides," he says, noting that his district has a large number of economically disadvantaged students who don't own computing devices.

"They're going to benefit by more technology being available, or perhaps benefit by being in a group of four or five students where somebody brought their own device," he says. "Perhaps that device could potentially act as the conduit out to the web at large to get information for a group. So it could benefit more than just the owner of the piece of equipment.

"I just don't see how we can, for a whole lot longer, simply deny the presence of a device that could enhance and expand the instructional process for no real good reason, other than we're just not sure about what would happen. And I think we owe it to ourselves to at least try it."

SIX

Bring-Your-Own-Laptop Programs Are Complicated but Worthwhile

Eamonn O'Donovan

Eamonn O'Donovan is a school administrator who lives in California. In this viewpoint, written from his experience as principal of a kindergarten-through-eighth-grade school that had instituted a program involving the use of laptops at school, O'Donovan questions whether the laptop program is worthwhile. He notes that scores on standardized tests did not improve as a result of the program. He suggests that one-to-one laptop programs do have benefits, however, and might be more effective in schools that already have higher test scores. He suggest several guidelines for school administrators who are considering such a program, including establishing methods for measuring the effectiveness of the program, tying the program to the curriculum, and working closely with students, teachers, parents, and the community.

I opened the doors of a brand new, state-of-the-art K–8 school in Orange County, Calif., in September 2003. As principal, I spearheaded an initiative to place as many laptop computers in the hands of students in grades 3–8 as possible. The goal was to prepare these students for a technology-driven world in which innovation, creativity, autonomy, and individual and group research was prized along with the traditional accumulation of knowledge. The idea was to help them to become problem-solvers who could use an ever-expanding and ever-changing base of knowledge to apply learning in task-oriented scenarios. These are the skills prized by the U.S. economy.

We did not have the funding to provide a computer for every student. California did not embrace this concept, as other states have done, and now does not have the resources, given the current state of school finances. Instead, the school provided as many computers as possible, up to five per classroom, and a number of roving laptop labs. The gap was filled by parents in a voluntary program in which students brought a laptop from home to use in class.

Within two years, about 60 percent of students had brought a laptop from home to use at school. With an instructional focus on project-type group learning, students were using computers during day-to-day instruction and learning in a one-to-one computer environment. For example, seventh-grade science students conducted Internet research and made PowerPoint presentations and iMovies on the genetic components of Parkinson's disease, ADHD, and other conditions. Students were motivated and engaged, and deep learning was taking place.

As a site administrator, I was faced with a broad array of challenges, many unique to a school that had to convince teachers and parents that learning with laptops was a viable and effective way to improve learning and instruction. Today these challenges have been amplified on two fronts, namely, spotty implementation of laptop programs in general and the attendant diminishing of support from teachers and parents, and a lack of hard data on the efficacy of the programs. With the substantial outlay of capital involved in these programs, policy makers are taking a harder look at laptop programs.

No Effect on Test Scores
When I first became involved in this project, the press for one-to-one computing was overwhelmingly positive. The initiative

"For those with books, open and follow along. For those with laptops, follow me on Twitter."

"For those with books, open and follow along. For those with laptops, follow me on Twitter," cartoon by Marty Bucella. www.CartoonStock.com.

was often a matter of policy from state or district leaders hoping to prepare students for an information-driven global economy. It was in essence a way to keep America competitive. Almost six years later, the tide has turned. A *New York Times* article from May 4, 2007, entitled "Seeing No Progress, Some Schools Drop Laptops" quoted policy makers as follows: "The teachers were telling us when there's a one-to-one relationship between the student and the laptop, the box gets in the way. It's a distraction to the educational process." Additionally, parents were frustrated that their children were spending too much time on video games. In other words, policy and theory did not pan out in practice, as teachers, students, and parents expressed pretty typical concerns with one-to-one laptop programs in actual classrooms.

The lack of data on the effect of laptop programs on standardized test scores is a significant Achilles heel. Simply stated, in my experience, laptop programs do not have a direct bearing on standardized test scores. This is borne out by research, scarce though it may be. For example, in a summary of the first-year implementation of the laptop program in Fullerton, Calif., researchers concluded that "students in the laptop program improved in test scores from the prior year at about the same rate as other students in the district." In other words, laptop programs do not raise test scores. As the pressure for achievement increases as No Child Left Behind [NCLB] pushes school systems to 100 percent student proficiency by 2014, it is becoming increasingly difficult to justify expenditures that do not have an impact on the bottom line of improving student achievement, at least as it is measured on state accountability systems.

Advocates for learning with laptops would say that you can't measure effectiveness with traditional measures of student performance, as it's a mismatch in skill sets. In fact, I often told parents if you ask how laptops improve test scores, you are asking the wrong question. However, laptop programs have yet to come up with a way to measure efficacy, and principals and schools are evaluated on standardized test scores. In fact, if your goal as an administrator is to raise test scores with laptops alone, you will likely fail.

As a further blow, research from the U.S. Department of Education published in 2007 on the effectiveness of reading and math software concluded that there was no measurable difference between the use of software and traditional methods.

What does this mean for implementing a one-to-one laptop program, especially in today's climate of increased accountability and diminishing resources? It depends upon the circumstances of individual schools.

If you are in program improvement or close to program improvement under NCLB, laptop programs will not help you to raise the basic skills of students. You don't have the time to wait to see if the program will work; you need results now. If your school has good test scores, has effectively implemented research-based instructional methods in reading and math, and has a supportive local community, however, a laptop program may help you to get to the next level.

Monitoring Is Necessary

If you are considering implementing or continuing a laptop program, it is important to recognize the importance of the site administrator in the process and the pressures that he or she will face. The principal will always have to justify the program with data, so an effective monitoring program will have to be established. This is traditionally an area where laptop programs have fallen down. In the absence of compelling data from the school, it makes it all the harder to resist the pressure from the story that standardized test scores tell.

In a policy brief from Andrew Zucker, senior research scientist at the Concord Consortium, entitled "One-to-One Computing Evaluation Consortium," published in November 2005, Bette Manchester states, "There needs to be a leadership team that looks at things through three different lenses: the lens of curriculum and content; the lens of the culture of the building; and the lens of technical needs." I believe this is an effective organizational framework with which to plan, implement, and evaluate a one-to-one laptop program.

Laptop Standards Have to Support Curriculum

Too often, instructional fads, in which laptop programs are sometimes included, forget to focus on the area of curriculum and content. Whatever the instructional practice, it must support the intended curriculum. One of the key components to improving student learning is to clearly identify what it is that students are expected to learn. Laptop programs have to support the standards that students are expected to master. Therefore, the focus should be on learning content standards. Schools may add goals in problem solving and critical thinking, but these must be pursued using instructional practices that are grounded in the content standards.

Laptop computers can be one important element in an instructional approach that can meet these standards as well as goals like innovation, creativity, and research. For example, if a grade level team identifies the key content or power standards for a learning unit, develops a set of essential questions that guide learning and assessment, and then uses laptops as one part of the instructional program, students will make progress that can be measured on standardized tests while acquiring the skills needed for the workplace of the future.

Guidelines Need to Be Established

Site administrators, with their leadership teams, must create a culture that is receptive to the use of laptop computers as learning tools. In addition, they must address the needs and interests of the key stakeholders in the learning community.

Students. Parents often say that their kids seem to spend an awful lot of time playing games or doing other nonacademic activities on their laptops. Therefore, at each school, it is important to establish clear guidelines for the use of laptops by students during classroom time. These expectations must be taught explicitly and reinforced positively as part of the normal process for establishing expected behaviors in all areas of school life. Students take to technology like ducks to water and have never known a world without the Internet. Learning with computers is natural for them; you just have to guide it to positive outcomes, an important ancillary goal of laptop programs in itself.

Teachers. It is difficult for teachers to change practices without extensive and ongoing staff development in the area of technology. This has two components: It is important to establish a baseline of proficiency with the technology itself. However, this is secondary to helping teachers to use laptops as instructional tools. If teachers do not actively plan for the use of laptops in the classroom, students will not bring them to class. The principal has to plan for ongoing training that mixes direct instruction, mentoring and coaching, and the sharing of best practices. This can only be achieved if the school has built staff development into the weekly

Middle school students work on laptops together. According to the author, laptop programs can be worthwhile, but it is critical that educators develop very specific guidelines for their use.

schedule at the school. One-time or sporadic in-services will not work; the push has to be constant, with clearly stated expectations for the use of technology as a learning tool. Fortunately, new textbook adoptions have strong online components with support provided by the publishers, and this will encourage teachers to tread further into the waters of technology and learning.

Parents. It is important to educate parents on the goals of the laptop program and to describe for them how students and teachers will use laptops, how learning will take place, and how the school will evaluate the success of the program. It is also important to identify potential pitfalls, like inappropriate student use of the Internet, for example, and to explain how the school will address them. This was critically important in my case, as I had the added pressure of having to justify the program for parents who purchased laptops for their children to bring to school. There will be rocky moments as parents have to put their own money on the line to buy laptops, purchase low-cost leases, or upgrade or repair computers. Many laptop schools have parent education nights to show how children will use the computers. Further education should include teaching parents how to use some of the software used in the program and how to solve problems and address basic computer glitches related to Internet access and printing documents.

Community. It is vital to establish business partnerships to build support for the laptop program. This can bring additional resources and good word of mouth about your program. At my school, we entered into a partnership with the local Apple Store. Our program grew over time to be mutually beneficial: Parents bought computers at the store, and Apple employees loaded the standard software needed for the school program as part of the purchase. . . .

Computers will continue to offer enticing opportunities for learning in our classrooms. The concept of "right now" learning is particularly powerful, as students find information as they need or request it. As computers decline in price and improve in functionality, laptop programs will continue to deliver on the promise of "anywhere, anytime learning." Our students will certainly enter a workplace that will be unrecognizable to us, and we will need to equip them with the skills to embrace and manage change in how information is produced, delivered and received. In the end, the key elements in a laptop program at school will continue to be the teacher-student relationship and the integration of technology, curriculum content, and school culture.

SEVEN

Laptops Should Be Banned from Classrooms

Timothy Snyder

> Timothy Snyder is a professor of history at Yale University. In this viewpoint, he explains why he does not allow students to use laptops in class. He describes ways that laptops can be distracting, even when students are using them to find out more about the subject he is lecturing on. Snyder believes that students should learn from the spoken word, and that students' grades are better when they use their laptops only outside of class.

As these first few weeks of the [fall 2010] college semester begin, professors look out expectantly into grand lecture halls, where they see, rather than faces of students, the backs of open laptops. The students, for their part, are looking intently at the laptop screens. What are they doing as they stare forward with such apparent focus?

Thanks to wireless Internet access, they are updating their Facebook, Twitter, and Tumblr profiles; they are chatting on Skype, Gchat, or iChat; they are making travel plans, or reading the newspaper, or following the pennant race. This fall, higher education lost yet another new class of freshmen, as the new students learned that the university classroom is just one more physical place to be on the Internet.

I teach at Yale, where lecturing is taken seriously—and in history, which boasts some of the best teachers. My ratings as a lecturer are consistently high. But even here, I would not have the attention of these very gifted students if I did not ban laptops and smartphones from my classroom. Part of the problem is that

Critics of using laptops in schools say students cannot resist the temptation to go online to chat or surf instead of paying attention to classwork.

students are not paying attention at a given moment; part of the problem is that they often lack the ability to pay attention at all.

Of course, some of them think they are paying attention: The well-intentioned are checking the professor's facts by googling. This is not a good use of that powerful tool, because what they learn in the class comes only from the class, and has a richness and precision they won't get online. Once the search happens, the students miss the next minute of lecture, or even more, as they then follow the next appealing link. It doesn't take long to get from googling Habermas to reading about Lady Gaga.

Laptops Are a Distraction

Almost none of my colleagues have any sense of the scale of the problem. To most professors over 50, the computer is an educational tool. If a student asked a professor for permission to bring a television set to class, the professor would be shocked. But a laptop connected to the Internet is, among other things, a television set. During lectures, students at our very best schools watch TV shows, video clips, and movies on YouTube, Hulu, or Vimeo. The forest of laptops may look much better than a television set on every desk, but in fact, it's far worse.

In the beginning, about 15 years ago, students really did just use their laptops to take notes. But step by step, and so imperceptibly, we have moved to a situation where even the students who want to take notes are distracted by their own screens and those of their neighbors. The one devoted student using pen and paper is also distracted by the glow and flash, and the noise of fingers on keypads. It's hard, as a student at another Ivy League school told me, to keep the focus after forty-five minutes of hard work when one neighbor has a music video going and the other is checking his stocks on line.

Learning Directly from Another Human

Meanwhile, we are losing the long tradition of people learning from other people. The lecture course, in one form or another, has been around for more than 2,000 years. The ability of one human being to reach another by speech is an irreplaceable part of what it means to be human. In seminars, laptops are still more harmful, serving as physical barriers that prevent a group of students from becoming a class.

Even more concerning, after university, students who could not concentrate in the classroom will become workers who cannot concentrate in the workplace. It is possible that the American economy will never out-compete others because we have the most easily distracted workforce.

Removing Laptops from Classrooms Improves Focus

Removing laptops from the classroom gives students a chance to focus, and a chance to learn to focus. Without the flash of

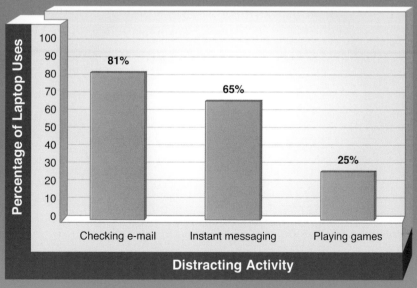

Students Use Laptops for Distracting Activities During Class

A Winona State University study showed that significant percentages of students use laptops for distracting activities in class.

Percentage of Laptop Uses

- Checking e-mail: 81%
- Instant messaging: 65%
- Playing games: 25%

Distracting Activity

Taken from: Kara Star, "New Study Shows Laptop Use in Class May Hurt," *Flat Hat* (College of William and Mary, Williamsburg, VA), February 23, 2007.

screens and the sound of typing, they find themselves—learning. In most courses, much is lost and nothing is gained by the use of the Internet. If the students need to use the Internet, they have the remaining 23 hours of the day, and indeed the rest of their lives, to do their screen-staring.

College students who spend their time online are missing out not only on education, but on experience. The four years of university are probably the best part of American life. It seems a shame to spend that time doing something that can be done anywhere and at any time. By allowing students to spend class time on the Internet, we professors are sending the message that college is just one more backdrop for googling.

And what do the students think? Almost all of them, judging from the student evaluations of my previous courses, saw the logic of the laptop ban, and liked the atmosphere of calm and concentration that it permitted. If, at some future point, the tide of student opinion turns against me, I have one final argument: Ever since the laptop ban was inaugurated, my students have been earning far better grades.

EIGHT

Schools Should Ban Cell Phones

Eric Novak

Eric Novak is an editor and video producer residing in Ajax, Ontario. In this viewpoint, he talks about a decision that the Toronto District School Board made to revoke a ban on cell phones and other electronic devices in the classroom. Novak argues that classrooms are for learning and that having phones in the classroom hinders learning, especially when students are texting instead of paying attention in class.

Earlier today, the Toronto District School Board (TDSB)—the largest school board in Canada—decided to rescind a 4 year old ban that prohibited cell phones and other personal electronic devices from classrooms and hallways at all of its schools. The ban will be removed as of September [2011] and will instead, place the responsibility of deciding what is considered appropriate and what is inappropriate use of these devices to individual teachers.

A Double-Edged Sword

Let me tell you why I think this decision to rescind the ban is wrong. Without question, the world that we live in today is substantially different than that of even one generation earlier. My children always glaze over and look at me with disbelief when I tell them about how computers were very basic and just entering our schools when I was a kid. They are stunned to hear that the internet wasn't even created until I had earned my Bachelor's Degree and that e-mail, cell phones, laptops and many other personal electronic creature comforts simply didn't exist when I was in school. I learned to type on something called a typewriter, which apparently is now only viewable to kids while on display at museums. I get and fully understand that personal technology has made tremendous advances and the way we conduct our lives is fundamentally different because of it.

What I also understand is these same technological advancements carry with them a double-edged sword. The pros and cons of technology is a subject we could write volumes about, but for the purpose of this post I'm simply going to focus on the pros and cons of technology and schools. When I went to high school in the 1980's we had Walkmans and other personal cassette players. We played music and listened to them with headphones. They were a form of entertainment for the most part for all we could do with them was play music. Nowadays kids play music on little [iPods] and MP3 players that store hundreds of songs on them. They can also store music on personal smartphones and cell phones which every teenager now seems to carry around. With the advent of text messaging these phones have become so much more than phones. They are modes of communication which can be utilized at any given moment and Canadians for example have gone nuts about texting.

Rapidly Changing Technology

Yesterday I saw a new story that showed how in 2010 Canadians sent 56.4 billion text messages. It's equivalent to 154.5 million texts per day and it's a number that is up an incredible 60% when compared to 2009. A big surge in this number comes from our youth. Teens for example seem to have adopted texting as the de facto way to communicate with their peers. Given that one doesn't have to speak or be heard to send a text message, the

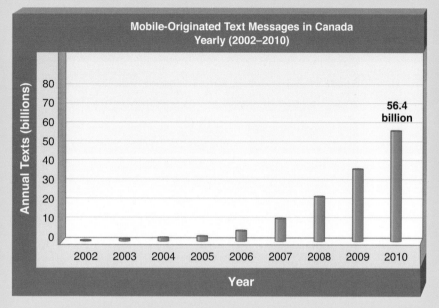

Taken from: Ian Hardy, "CWTA Canadians Sent 56.4 Billion Text Messages in 2010," www.mobilesyrup.com, May 16, 2011. Data from Canadian Wireless Telecommunications Association (CWTA).

ability to send these messages regardless of where they are is certainly one of its big draws to youth. Four years ago the TDSB implemented a ban on cellphones and other personal electronic devices because they saw an increase in the amount of texting taking place during class time. It was meant to minimize distractions and to keep the student's attentions focused on the teacher and the lessons being learned.

Those who have argued against the ban and in favour of its removal claim that we live in a different world where cell phones serve many purposes and to prohibit them from even being in the halls and classrooms is unfair. I was advised by someone that this also included things like laptops and tablets which could be used during study periods but were lumped in with cell phones and banned as well. I responded to him that while I can see how the banning of laptops and tablets may not be right, the ban on cell

Critics of cell phones in class say that because kids use texting as a primary means of communication, the phones serve only to distract students in the classroom.

phones should still be in place. The right thing for the Board to have done would have been to amend the ban instead of removing it completely to allow for laptops and tablets but still restrict cell phones.

Not the Place for Cell Phones

A classroom is a place of learning. Learning happens best when attention is focused on the lesson at hand and not when partially on the lesson and partially on reading what everyone is doing after class. To make the rules now subjective and at the discretion of the teachers now creates a situation where anyone who wants to keep the ban in place will eventually succumb to the tide initiated by those who are either not willing to or not prepared to tell their students to keep phones off.

Some parents argue that they need to be able to communicate with their children at all times in case of an emergency. Well, when I went to school if my Mom needed to reach me, she called the school office and the office called my teacher. The funny thing is that this still works today and is just as effective as it was back then. In fact I would argue that a parent who feels compelled to text their child while the child is in class, is doing their child a disservice unless there is absolutely something of critical importance to share for it causes them to not pay attention to the lesson and to pay attention instead to them.

If a school is a place designed to prepare our kids for adult and professional life, then allowing cellphones to be on in class contradicts many professional business practices currently in place. I have attended many business networking events or seminars and the rules of courtesy always state that cellphones should be turned off. In fact many organizations have begun instituting penalties, such as $10 paid directly to charity for anyone caught using their phones or taking a call during an event. Focusing on the presenter or the event and not on your texts, e-mails or BBMs [BlackBerry messages] is a matter of courtesy and very few people wind up being fined because they understand that there is a time and a place for everything.

In our society we tend to easily get confused between what is a right and what is a privilege. Access to food and clean water is a right. Access to cell phones is a privilege and there must be a clear distinction between the two. Cell phones DO NOT belong in classrooms and I hope that other school boards across the country *will not* follow the lead established by the myopic and misguided decision of the Toronto District School Board.

NINE

Cell Phones Can Be Learning Tools Instead of Distractions

William M. Ferriter

William M. Ferriter teaches sixth-grade language arts and social studies in Raleigh, North Carolina. In this viewpoint, he argues that teachers should make use of cell phones in classrooms. He suggests curtailing irresponsible behaviors by bringing cell phones out into the open and requiring that they be placed on top of the desk. Using Poll Everywhere, an online polling site that uses text messaging, as an example, he encourages teachers to look for applications that are useful in the classroom. He also applauds the use of cell phones to replace expensive classroom items such as cameras and dictionaries.

At a recent conference, a team of teachers asked me an all-too-common question: How can we get the educators in our building to embrace cell phones as a legitimate tool for learning? The teachers told me cell phones were banned by school policy—and most of their colleagues wouldn't have it any other way.

Sound familiar? Despite the fact that 75 percent of all kids ages 12–17 have cell phones, educators have done their best to aggressively erase this tool from their classrooms. In fact, less than 12 percent of students attend schools where cell phones can be accessed at any time—and almost 70 percent attend schools where cell phones are banned from the classroom.

Don't get me wrong: Our efforts to control student cell phone use are—at times—noble. Cell phones can be a real disruption to learning when used improperly. With almost 60 percent of teens reporting that they've sent and received text messages and 25 percent reporting that they've made phone calls *while in class*, the disruptions are real.

But efforts to eliminate cell phone use are also short-sighted, especially in an era when fewer dollars are available for classroom supplies. With a willingness to experiment, teachers might be able to create classrooms where the cell phones currently tucked into students' backpacks function as important tools instead of incessant distractions.

How to Make Cell Phones Useful

To break down negative attitudes toward cell phones as learning tools in your building, try the following.

1. Make cell phones visible. Most cell phone skeptics I know are worried about sneaky students. "What if my kids text answers to one another during tests?" they'll argue. My solution is simple: Require students to place their cell phones on the top right-hand corner of their desks when they come into class. That way you will know if someone is texting or calling a friend when they're supposed to be learning.

The best answer to students who act irresponsibly with cell phones isn't a blanket ban (which they'll probably ignore anyway). The best answer is to force students to act responsibly.

2. Show colleagues and administrators one convincing classroom application. Convincing educators to embrace any new tool starts with demonstrating how it can improve learning or make our work easier—show us that, and we'll embrace almost anything. To make a case for cell phones, you might demonstrate a text-messaging-based polling system like Poll Everywhere, which allows users to create surveys that participants respond to via text messaging.

Majority of Teens Can Have Phones at School but Not in Class

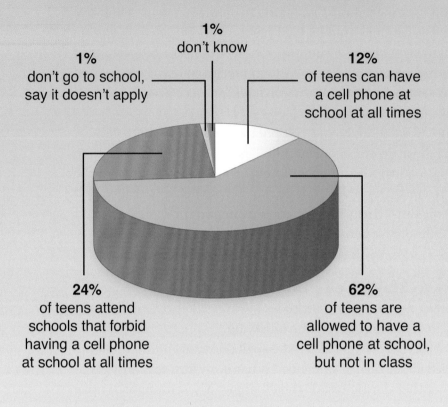

1%
don't know

1%
don't go to school,
say it doesn't apply

12%
of teens can have
a cell phone at
school at all times

24%
of teens attend
schools that forbid
having a cell phone
at school at all times

62%
of teens are
allowed to have a
cell phone at school,
but not in class

Taken from: Amanda Lenhart, "Teens & Mobile Phones," Pew Internet & American Life Project, October 2010.

By creating an account (free for groups of 30 or less) on Poll Everywhere's website (www.polleverywhere.com), you set your class up as a polling group. You'll instantly have the capacity to create brief multiple-choice or open-answer surveys that you can show in class using a data projector. Students can then text their responses—either as short answers or pre-determined codes automatically assigned to each indicator of a multiple-choice question—back to Poll Everywhere. Results are displayed instantly for the entire class to see, are updated in real time, and can be downloaded for future reference. (I've found that my class members are happy to share their phones with those few students who aren't carrying a cell phone or don't have a texting plan.)

Poll Everywhere turns cell phones into student responders—something most schools can't afford—that teachers can use to gather information about content mastery in their class. For instance, science teachers curious about whether their students can accurately convert metric measurements into standard measurements can create quick multiple-choice surveys with Poll Everywhere and instantly see how well their students grasp the content and conversion procedures presented in class. Considering how important efficiently collecting data has become in today's classroom—and that 75 percent of all students with cell phones have unlimited texting plans—services like Poll Everywhere should be an instant hit in most schools.

Replacing School Supplies

3. *Use cell phones to replace needed supplies.* I first became convinced that cell phones had a place in the classroom when my students were completing a science lab that required timing the melting rate of an ice cube. Students were excited by the lab, but we didn't have enough timers for every group. "Can I use the timer on my cell phone?" a student asked. "Sure," I said, pleasantly surprised. I hadn't even realized cell phones had timers.

Over time, cell phones filled many functions in my classroom. Students looking for definitions to new terms or answers to basic knowledge questions started texting their questions—What is the capital of Cuba? What is the definition of *onomatopoeia*? What is the speed of sound?—to Google's dedicated SMS question service number and receiving instant replies. Students also began using the still and video camera features of their cell phones to record the results of their labs for future review and to insert photographs of procedures and materials into lab reports.

Think of the money we saved! Using nothing more than the tools that the majority of students brought to school every day, we'd successfully replaced dictionaries, timers, and digital

Some schools are using cell phones as instructional tools. This teacher is texting messages in Spanish to her Spanish language class.

cameras—resources my principal would have loved to provide for every classroom, but couldn't afford in tight budget times.

Embracing cell phones in schools is a logical step. Although the risks are real, the rewards are great—and not as hard to achieve as you might think.

TEN

Texting Is a Distraction from Learning

Patrick Welsh

> Patrick Welsh is an English teacher at T.C. Williams High School in Alexandria, Virginia, and a regular contributor to *USA Today*. In this viewpoint, he discusses his views on text messaging, especially in the classroom. Welsh believes that texting is a distraction that prohibits students from concentrating on learning, and he recommends that parents and teachers should not allow children to use text messaging or to bring their phones to school.

When students graduate from T.C. Williams High School in Alexandria, Va., on Thursday [June 25, 2009], school officials will do what they should have done back in September: Take possession of all the iPods and cellphones. As students go into the graduation ceremony, they will be searched and their electronic toys will be taken away. At a meeting of some 560 seniors a few weeks ago, the principal told them that they "could live without their cellphones for two hours."

He might have been a bit presumptuous. The iPods are bad enough. Every day, students—between and often during class—are plugged into their iPods, seemingly off in another world.

But it's cellphone text messaging that both parents and schools need to declare war on. Texting has become an obsession with teenagers around the country. According to the Nielsen Co., in the last quarter of 2008, teens were averaging at least 80 texts a day, a figure double what it was the year before.

T.C. Williams' handbook for parents boldly declares, "The operation of electronic devices including cellphones and iPods is not permitted in the school building. These items will be confiscated for a minimum of 24 hours on the first offense."

Reality, though, is something else. The rules are so inconsistently enforced that kids consider them more an inconvenience than a real threat. Even parents send text messages to their kids during class time.

And the problem is getting worse, as students become more adept at disguising their texting. One student admitted to often sending 10 texts during my class. Others admitted to sending and receiving more than 200 texts over the course of a day. Most kids are such pros that they can text while the phone is in their pocket, a purse or under the desk, while maintaining eye contact with the teacher.

For the most part, all this subterfuge might seem like innocent adolescent behavior, but evidence suggests that texting is undermining students' ability to focus and to learn—and creating anxiety to boot.

Essential to Students' Lives

Many students have come to feel that they cannot live without texting. Says senior Laura Killalea, with a hint of hyperbole: "Most of my friends would die if they had to go to school without their cellphones." Another student, Yasir Hussein, admits that when he doesn't have his phone he gets anxious. "I feel like I am in the dark, secluded, isolated." Cellphones have taken such control over teens that virtually all the students I talked to said they often feel as if their phones are vibrating when they don't even have them.

MIT professor Sherry Turkle told me that texting is "an always-on/always-on-you technology." She says cellphones cause not only "the anxiety of disconnection," but also "the anxiety of con-

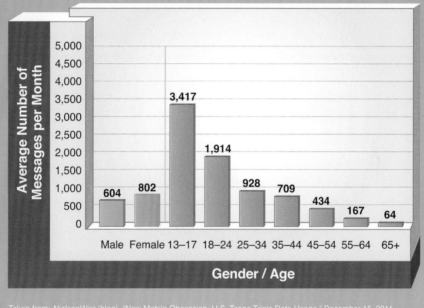

Average Number of Messages Exchanged per Month, Third Quarter, 2011

When using their mobile phones, US teens prefer messaging over calling, saying it is faster, easier, and more enjoyable.

Average Number of Messages per Month

Gender / Age	Value
Male	604
Female	802
13–17	3,417
18–24	1,914
25–34	928
35–44	709
45–54	434
55–64	167
65+	64

Taken from: *NielsenWire* (blog), "New Mobile Obsession: U.S. Teens Triple Data Usage," December 15, 2011. http://blog.nielsen.com/nielsenwire/online_mobile/new-mobile-obsession-u-s-teens%20triple-data-usage.

nection which comes from the expectation that you will respond immediately to a message you get."

Despite all the technological advances that ere intended to increase communication and efficiency, adolescents as well as adults are living in what Maggie Jackson, author of *Distracted: The Erosion of Attention and the Coming Dark Age*, calls "an institutionalized culture of interruption, where our time and attention is being fragmented by a never-ending stream of phone calls, e-mails, instant messages, text messages and tweets."

For students, these "advancements" only add to the difficulties an already distracted generation has had maintaining focus to do serious school work. "Attention is at the heart of any in-depth intellectual activity. When your times of focus and reflection are always being punctured by a cellphone buzzing, it's hard to go deeply into thinking and problem solving. You cannot be creative," says Jackson. "Texting is undermining kids' opportunities to learn. . . . They will shy away from challenging material."

Although texting is a convenient method of instant communication, it requires such brevity that, according to the author, it worsens students' writing abilities.

One of the great ironies of the high-tech revolution is that devices meant to facilitate communication are actually helping to destroy it. For my students, rethinking what they wrote and hammering out second or third drafts is beyond all but a handful. In fact, texting has a language all its own, with its own abbreviations and terse messages, all of which hardly translates into good writing.

Math and science teachers at my school see the same, with kids wanting the quick answers instead of going through the struggle that will help them understand what is behind the mathematical or scientific principles involved.

Stop Children from Texting

Even so, there is hope.

"We have fallen into bad habits with all the new technology," Jackson says, "but we can push back on the distractions, control those habits. We need to look at it all with fresh eyes, tally up the cost that distraction is costing us and our children and make changes."

The summer break is upon us, but administrators and parents need to consider two changes before students return in the fall:

- Parents should disable the text messaging function of their kids' cellphones.
- Those students who curse teachers out and refuse to hand over their phones—as has happened often at T.C. Williams—will have to be punished. A crackdown the first day of school in September will set the get-tough tone for the rest of the year.

At the very least, administrators and parents can agree that the school day should be the one time when kids can do without their cellphones. Or maybe I'm just being presumptuous.

ELEVEN

Cell Phones in the Classroom May Lead to Secretly Created Videos

Vaishali Honawar

In this viewpoint, journalist Vaishali Honawar discusses a number of incidents where students have used cell phones to make video recordings of their teachers—without the teachers' knowledge—and then posted the videos on YouTube and other online sites. She highlights some of the problems this can cause for the teacher, from embarrassment to professional discipline, depending on what the teacher is doing in the video. She notes some of the controversy around whether or not cell phones should be allowed in the classroom and suggests that parents, teachers, and school administrators need to discuss policies around secret video recordings made of teachers.

Videos of teachers that students taped in secrecy are all over online sites like YouTube and MySpace. Angry teachers, enthusiastic teachers, teachers clowning around, singing, and even dancing are captured, usually with camera phones, for the whole world to see. Some students go so far as to create elaborately edited videos that use popular soundtracks and sound effects to poke fun at their teachers. Now, concern is growing among teacher advocates that the proliferation of such videos is causing stress for teachers and some students, and could have a chilling effect on classroom discussions.

"It is disturbing to the educational process," said David Strom, the general counsel for the American Federation of Teachers (AFT), because the fear of being taped could change how teachers interact with students. What's more, the trend could deter class participation by students "who wouldn't want to speak up for fear of being mocked, if they felt their answers would be put up on the Internet," Strom said.

Consequences for Teachers

The threat of exposure by cell phone cameras has potential professional, as well as emotional, consequences for teachers. A teacher in Arizona was placed on administrative leave last month [January 2008], pending an investigation, after doing a cheerleading routine in class. Some students later said that she had performed the routine at their request and that they had not found it offensive.

In another well-publicized case, in the Kent school district in Washington State, teacher Joyce Mong found herself the subject of a video titled "Mongzilla," shot by students that made fun of her appearance.

Almost every teacher interviewed for this article had a story to tell. Teacher-written blogs are replete with tales of students' using now ubiquitous—and easily concealed—communications devices in class to take videos or still pictures.

Jay Rehak, an English teacher at Whitney Young High School in Chicago, said that he would be willing to have parents or others sit in his class and observe. But it worries him that someone might take a small slice of a 45-minute class and put a misleading video on the Web.

He recalls that a colleague became irate in class and was surreptitiously taped by a student. The video wound up on YouTube. "I wouldn't appreciate it if it happened to me. . . . Everybody makes

Because cell phones allow students to film teachers secretly and to post the videos on the Internet, teachers fear that such videos can cause their comments to be taken out of context and/or misinterpreted.

mistakes," Rehak said. "Anyone can take a clip of anyone at the wrong time and make it look really bad."

Paul Martin, a teacher at the private AGBU Manoogian-Demirdjian School in Canoga Park, CA, said a student once taped him with a cell phone while he was teaching, and the video was posted online. While there was nothing damaging in the video, just the experience of finding it online was unnerving because he had no clue he was being taped. "I went to the student and talked to him, and told him that I didn't have the expectation of being taped," said Martin. The student apologized.

A Global Concern

With the pervasive presence of the Internet and forums such as YouTube, a free video-sharing site where users can upload and view video clips, it is not surprising that the issue resonates around the globe. Teacher videos can be found online from Canada to South Korea. Teachers in those other countries have also raised their voices in protest against the student videos.

In Britain, a teachers' union last year called for a ban on YouTube, accusing the company of encouraging cyber-bullying. In a case in Scotland cited in the *Guardian* newspaper, students filmed a teacher in the classroom and posted it on YouTube with the caption "You are dead." YouTube eventually took the video down.

In Quebec, Canada, four students were suspended after they taped a teacher yelling at a student.

In Finland, a student was found guilty of libel and ordered to pay 800 euros in damages by a court for putting a video online of a teacher singing with karaoke accompaniment at a school party. The video was labeled "karaoke of the mental hospital."

Schools Ignore Embarrassing Videos

Here in the United States, legal experts say school districts tend to ignore videos that are simply embarrassing to a teacher. They do act when they find that the taping is a threat to the school or teacher or is disruptive to learning.

"There are a variety of issues with cell phones in school and what's been posted," said Tom Hutton, a senior staff attorney for the National School Boards Association (NSBA), based in Alexandria, VA. "Did students make comments that were threatening? Was it a threat or was it a parody?" Districts tend to be more concerned when they see safety issues around a student-posted teacher video. Legal experts say they are unaware of any instances in which a teacher filed a lawsuit against a student and his or her family because of a video.

Teachers could potentially sue for defamation if someone selectively made recordings to cast them in a libelous light, the AFT's

Strom said. He also pointed out that laws in several states prohibit recording a person without his or her knowledge.

Teachers' Legal Rights Are Unclear

What complicates the issue for teachers who find themselves the unwitting subjects of their students' handiwork are court precedents that can be interpreted to mean that teachers do not have privacy rights in a classroom.

Thomas E. Wheeler II, an Indianapolis-based lawyer who is on the board of directors of the NSBA's Council of School Attorneys, points to two lawsuits. In *Evens v. L.A. Unified School District*, students covertly taped a teacher's classroom performance that was later used against her in termination proceedings. The court held that a teacher must always expect public dissemination of his or her classroom communications and activities.

In *Roberts v. Houston Independent School District*, the court found that videotaping a teacher's classroom performance by a school did not violate the teacher's privacy rights. Schools could potentially act in cases where they found that students used school equipment to tape or to put videos online, Wheeler said, or if a video proved substantially disruptive to the school or the learning process.

"If a kid has a photo and posts it on YouTube, modified or unmodified, it is hard for the school to show disruption because of it. That's First Amendment speech," he said. He added that in districts or schools that require students to turn off cell phones, students could be subject to discipline for breaking that rule.

In the case of the videotaping of Mong, the offending student was suspended, but not for his online criticism of his teacher. Instead, he was punished for the disruption that he and his collaborators caused by bringing a video camera into her class.

Some Schools Ban Cell Phones

Districts have for years attempted to regulate the use of electronic pagers and then cell phones in schools because they can be disruptive and now, with the advent of the camera phones, are sometimes used to copy tests.

Most districts require students to turn cell phones off in classrooms. Some, New York City among them, bar students from bringing cell phones into classrooms. Such bans have attracted the wrath of parents, some of whom sued New York last year. The ban was upheld by a state court.

In Dallas, elementary students are not allowed to carry compact phones. Those in middle and high school have to turn their phones off during school hours. Spokeswoman Sandra Guerrero said that if a student was found using a cell phone, the teacher could take it away. Repeat offenses could cause a student to lose his cell phone, after which he would have to pay a $25 fine to retrieve it.

Other districts allow schools to make their own rules. For instance, in Chicago, schools are allowed to set their own policies on students' cell phone use.

In the District of Columbia, schools are free to set their own rules, and have come up with interesting ways to deal with the issue. At Benjamin Banneker High School, for instance, a neighborhood grocery store allows students to drop off their cells before they enter school.

Teacher Contracts Should Offer Protection

Teachers like Chicago's Rehak say that rules regulating cell phones are not enough. School districts need to include specific guidelines in their student-discipline codes forbidding their use to photograph teachers.

One option, said Strom, the AFT lawyer, is for unions to bargain for protections in their contracts. "It is conceivable that . . . a local union could bargain that if a student takes a video in the classroom, the district would investigate and take disciplinary action against the student."

Many contracts already include provisions on when and why teachers are videotaped by administrators for evaluation purposes. Districts and teachers have sometimes worked with YouTube and other host sites to remove particularly offensive videos, Strom added.

The Importance of Raising Awareness

As classrooms and students go more high tech, a need exists to start a conversation between parents—who want children to have cell phones for emergencies—and teachers and administrators on students' photographing of teachers on the sly, said John Wright, the president of the Arizona NEA [National Education Association]. The pros and cons of new technology in classrooms need to be thoroughly discussed to find a solution to the problem, Wright said.

Some teachers have found educating their students about the issue helpful. Kevin Metcalf teaches a Participation in Government class at North Rockland High School in Thiells, NY, in which he tries an experiment with his students. He asks them to whip out their cell phones—whose use is otherwise forbidden in the classroom under school rules—while he puts his head down on his desk for a second and acts as though he's doing nothing. He then asks them that if they were to take a picture and put it on YouTube, what would people think of his teaching?

"They come up with answers like 'lazy,' and 'doesn't care.' I say I would be judged by your peers on one second of a 45-minute class," he said. The experiment brings home to the students how such an action could misrepresent the truth and have serious consequences for someone.

Despite the lesson, Metcalf said, he knows a student could catch him on camera at any time. "My fear is one day I would be on a video," he said, "but, hopefully, it is something I could explain."

TWELVE

Electronic Communication Between Teachers and Students Raises Difficult Issues

Katie Ash

In this viewpoint, journalist Katie Ash discusses issues around policies regulating cyber-communication—such as e-mail and texting—between teachers and students. Ash describes how several school administrations have addressed this issue. Policies that ban all communication also prohibit positive interactions, such as sharing of homework assignments and discussions electronically. Policies that are too permissive or completely nonexistent leave open possibilities of inappropriate behavior. Some educators have concluded that a professional code of ethics and training for teachers about proper boundaries are more useful than policies specifying rules regarding particular technologies.

Teachers in Louisiana may soon think twice before sending a text message or e-mail to a student from a personal electronic device. A new state law requires all Louisiana districts to implement policies requiring documentation of every electronic interaction between teachers and students through a nonschool-issued device, such as a personal cellphone or e-mail account, by Nov. 15 [2009]. Parents also have the option of forbidding any communication between teachers and their child through personal electronic devices.

Similar policies exist in many school districts across the country, and at least one other state has considered such legislation in recent years. But critics question the measures, saying they will likely restrict appropriate communication between teachers and students and discourage the use of new technologies.

"The motivation for the bill was growing problems with [interactions] that started relatively innocently and escalated from there," said state Rep. Frank A. Hoffman, the Republican who wrote the bill, which Gov. Bobby Jindal signed into law in June [2009]. "It's to head something off before it ever gets started.

"We're not saying don't use [electronic devices], just that there should be a system of documentation," he said.

Determining what communications between teachers and students are appropriate, especially in the emerging fields of electronic devices and social-networking Web sites, is an issue that districts nationwide are navigating, with policies ranging from fairly permissive to more restrictive.

"We're at a point where [policies on this issue] are all over the map," said Ann Flynn, the director of education technology for the National School Boards Association, based in Alexandria, Va. "I think it is largely a local issue to be sorted out, ideally in a proactive [rather than reactive] way."

Unlike in Louisiana, such policies typically are determined locally, rather than at the state level, although similar legislation has appeared in the Missouri legislature, at least, but not been enacted.

A Negative Effect on Classroom Relations

Louisiana Rep. Walker Hines, a Democrat, voted against the bill in his state. "I did not believe that this legislation would deter any teacher from having a sexual relationship with a student," he

Electronic communications between teachers and students raise the difficult issue of how to avoid inappropriate communications without creating barriers to positive interactions.

said. "In fact, I believe this legislation could have a major chilling effect on teachers' becoming mentors for students."

For example, some teachers give out cellphone numbers to students who may have unstable home environments, Mr. Hines said. "Teachers [should be able to] give out their cellphone number," he said, "without any fear of unnecessary hassle or unintended consequences."

Ray Bernard, the child-welfare supervisor for the 15,000-student Lafourche Parish, La., public school system, believes the law provides enough flexibility to both protect students and keep legitimate teacher-student relationships intact.

The policy that his district will implement says that teachers, and all other school employees, must document any interaction through nonschool-issued electronic devices that happens with a student in that district, or any other district in the state, within 24 hours of the exchange.

The documentation consists of filling out an electronic form that explains the reason behind the interaction, which is then sent to the school administration. School employees are also expected to document occasions in which they are contacted by students through nonschool means. Those who violate the policy could be in danger of being fired, said Mr. Bernard.

"What we're hoping is that once [school employees] see the hassle that they have to go through to use their own communication device, then they'll . . . do it selectively, at best," he said.

The district's policy does not apply to one-way communication to groups of students regarding classroom assignments, such as a teacher posting homework instructions on a blog or Web page, Mr. Bernard said. The policy only refers to direct communication between individual students and school employees. The state law requires each school district to define electronic communication.

The Louisiana Association of Educators, an affiliate of the National Education Association, has released guidelines outlining what school policies on the matter could look like and how they should be carried out, said Joyce P. Haynes, the president of the state teachers' association. "We just see that it's like a necessary evil," she said of the new law's requirements. "Teachers jump through hoops all the time, and this is just another way of taking care of business."

Policy Can Focus on a Code of Ethics

In Texas, meanwhile, administrators in the 24,000-student McKinney Independent School District, north of Dallas, experienced an outcry from teachers, students, and parents after introducing a school policy that banned teacher-student communication through text messaging, e-mail, and social-networking Web sites.

The feedback "provided a lot of great examples of situations where [electronic exchanges like] texting became not only a valuable communication tool, but also sometimes a safety issue," said Cody Cunningham, a spokesman for the district.

School tennis coaches, for example, contended that texting was a valuable way of quickly reaching players who might be spread out over many courts, he said. The district was also informed of teachers who were using social-networking sites to provide educational content.

"When those concerns were raised, . . . we realized that maybe the decision to change our policy was done a little too quickly," Mr. Cunningham said, "and we decided to take more time to research what's an appropriate way to implement a policy that sets parameters, but also allows that opportunity for communication to occur."

In the end, the McKinney district's policy was revised to better reflect the needs of teachers and students, he said, by focusing more on a "professional code of ethics" than restrictions on specific technologies. "I think the intentions were good, but there was just a lack of understanding of all the implications," Mr. Cunningham said of the original policy.

The 8,600-student Lamar County school district in Purvis, Miss., received national attention when it implemented a policy last school year [2008–2009] that prohibits teachers from posting documents or photos online that "might result in a disruption of classroom activity" or interacting with students on social-networking sites.

"We want to keep the relationship between the teacher and the student on a professional basis," said Benjamin C. Burnett, the superintendent of the district. "We don't want to keep our teachers from building positive relationships with kids, but we want to make sure it's on an educational and professional level."

Since the Lamar County school system put its policy in place, many school districts in the surrounding area, as well as across the country, have gotten in touch with district officials because they plan to adopt similar policies, Mr. Burnett said.

Frequency of Text Messaging, by Age

Age	Text Hourly	Text Daily	Text Weekly	Never Text	All
15	7.02%	5.26%	1.75%	1.75%	15.79%
16	33.33%	26.32%	10.53%	0.00%	70.18%
17	7.02%	7.02%	0.00%	0.00%	14.04%

Taken from: Kevin Thomas and Corrie Orthober, "Using Text Messaging in the Secondary Classroom," *American Secondary Education*, Spring 2011, p.63.

The Challenge of Changing Technologies

Part of the challenge policymakers face when writing rules about teacher-student interactions through new technologies is the speed which with those technologies are emerging, said David S. Doty, the superintendent of the 33,000-student Canyons school district in Utah.

"Anybody dealing with young people will tell you that the law is not keeping pace with the evolution of technology, and the gap between those two seems to be getting bigger every year," said Mr. Doty, who also worked for 15 years as a lawyer. "It leaves school officials, frankly, dealing with a lot of this stuff on the fly," he said. "It's not because they're not prepared, . . . but because there really is not much formal guidance to help them."

The administration in the Canyons district is discussing what its policy to address teacher-student communications through electronic devices should entail. It does not currently have one in place. "At the end of the day, we depend on [teachers] to use good judgment," said Mr. Doty. "I don't think it's very effective to bring down this laundry list of 'thou shalt not.'"

In Utah, the state department of education requires each school district to have a policy, or have plans to implement a policy, that addresses teacher-student electronic communications, but it does not stipulate exactly what a policy should look like.

The department does provide two examples on its Web site of possible policies—one that is considered permissive, and one that is more restrictive.

Terri Miller, the president of the group Stop Educator Sexual Abuse, Misconduct, and Exploitation, based in Las Vegas, says policymakers should not enact "reactionary" legislation regarding contact between teachers and students. "What they really need to focus on is training in proper boundaries," Ms. Miller said. "You can pass laws . . . that prohibit inappropriate behavior between students and teachers, but that's not going to stop true predators."

What You Should Know About Electronic Devices in Schools

General Attitudes About Electronic Devices in Schools

A study by Blackboard K–12 called Learning in the 21st Century reports that:

- access to smartphones has more than tripled among high school students since 2006;
- students report that the primary barrier to using technology at school is the inability to use their own devices, such as cell phones, smartphones, MP3 players, laptops, or netbooks;
- 60 percent of middle school students and 64 percent of high school students prefer to use their own cell phone, smartphone, or MP3 player rather than a netbook or laptop;
- 62 percent of responding parents report that if their child's school allowed devices to be used for educational purposes, they would likely purchase a mobile device for their child;
- administrators report that the top barriers for implementing mobile devices in their schools and districts are the need for focused professional development for teachers and up-to-date policies related to network security.

Cell Phones at School

A 2010 Pew Internet and American Life study on teens and mobile phones found that:

- 12 percent of all students say they are allowed to have their phone at school at any time;
- 62 percent of all students say they are allowed have their phone in school, just not in class;
- 24 percent of teens attend schools that ban all cell phones from school grounds;
- 65 percent of teens who own cell phones and attend schools that completely ban phones bring their phones to school every day anyway;
- 58 percent of cellphone-owning teens at schools that ban phones have sent a text message during class;
- 43 percent of all teens who take their phones to school say they text in class at least once a day or more;
- 64 percent of teens with cell phones have texted in class, and 25 percent have made or received a call during class time.

One-to-One Device Programs

According to a 2008 study by The Greaves Group:

- Academic improvement results for one-to-one programs—in which each student has a laptop or similar device for use in the classroom—have climbed sharply. In 2006, 30 percent of districts reported moderate to significant improvement. In 2007, this number climbed to 78.7 percent.
- Slightly more than 27 percent of school districts report that they are involved in one-to-one computing.
- The average district pilot program has climbed to include 1,631 students; 40 percent of the district pilot programs include over a thousand students, and 10 percent include over five thousand students.
- Almost 31 percent of the district pilot programs involve three or more schools. These districts have moved beyond the initial stages and are on the path toward system-wide implementation.
- Only 7 percent of districts report that they are experiencing widespread technology problems with their one-to-one implementation.

What You Should Do About Electronic Devices in Schools

Gather Information

The first step in grappling with any complex and controversial issue is to be informed about it. Gather as much information as you can from a variety of sources. The essays in this book form an excellent starting point, representing a variety of viewpoints and approaches to the topic. Your school or local library will be another source of useful information; look there for relevant books, magazines, and encyclopedia entries. The bibliography and Organizations to Contact sections of this book will give you useful starting points in gathering additional information. Visit the websites of the organizations listed in the Organizations to Contact section to learn more.

Identify the Issues Involved

Once you have gathered your information, review it methodically to discover the key issues involved. Consider the pros and cons of using electronic devices in schools. Are there valid reasons for allowing devices in the classroom? Are there valid reasons for forbidding them? Is there a middle ground?

Evaluate Your Information Sources

As you learn about a topic, make sure to evaluate the sources of the information you have discovered. Authors always speak from their own perspective, which influences the way they perceive a subject and how they present information.

Consider the authors' experience and background. Are they educators? Students? Parents? Are they speaking from personal experience? Have they done research on the subject and gathered statistics? Someone with a personal perspective has a very different point of view from someone who has studied the issue at a distance. Both can be useful, but it is important to recognize what the author bases his or her opinion on.

Examine Your Own Perspective

Consider your own beliefs, feelings, and biases on this issue. Before you began studying, did you have an opinion about electronic devices in schools? If so, what influenced you to have this opinion—friends, family, personal experience, something you read or heard in the media? Be careful to acknowledge your own viewpoint and be willing to learn about other sides of the issue. Make sure to study and honestly consider opinions that are different from yours. Do they make some points that might convince you to change your mind? Do they raise more questions that you need to think about? Or does looking at other viewpoints more solidly convince you of your own initial perspective?

Form Your Own Opinion

Once you have gathered and organized information, identified the issues involved, and examined your own perspective, you will be ready to form your own opinion about electronic devices in schools and to advocate for that position. Whatever position you take, be prepared to explain it clearly on the basis of facts, evidence, and well-thought-out beliefs.

Take Action

Once you have developed your position on electronic devices in schools, you can consider turning your beliefs into action. Find out what your school's policy is and the reasons it was put into place. If you disagree with the policy, you can write a piece for your school paper explaining why you think the rule should be changed. You can also arrange to speak at a local PTA meeting and explain clearly and calmly how the rule could be changed.

You also might want to join an organization that shares your point of view—check out the Organizations to Contact section of this book for some starting points. These organizations offer ways that you can express your opinions or advocate for changes in school policies. If you would like to contact your political representatives directly to express your position on electronic devices in schools and what you think should be done, the website www.usa.gov /Contact/Elected.shtml can help you get started.

ORGANIZATIONS TO CONTACT

The editors have compiled the following list of organizations concerned with the issues debated in this book. The descriptions are derived from materials provided by the organizations. All have publications or information available for interested readers. The list was compiled on the date of publication of the present volume; names, addresses, phone and fax numbers, and e-mail and Internet addresses may change. Be aware that many organizations take several weeks or longer to respond to inquiries, so allow as much time as possible.

Association for the Advancement of Computing in Education (AACE)
PO Box 1545, Chesapeake, VA 23327-1545
(757) 366-5606
e-mail: info@aace.org
website: www.aace.org

AACE is an international educational and professional not-for-profit organization dedicated to the advancement of the knowledge, theory, and quality of learning and teaching at all levels with information technology. The purpose of AACE is accomplished through the encouragement of scholarly inquiry related to information technology in education and the dissemination of research results and their applications through publications, conferences, societies, and chapters, as well as interorganizational projects.

Center for Children & Technology (CCT)
96 Morton St., 7th Fl., New York, NY 10014
(212) 807-4200
e-mail: sp@edc.org
website: www.cct.edc.org

The CCT investigates ways that technology can make a difference in children's classrooms, schools, and communities through a number of research projects. Its goal is to construct a more complete understanding of how to foster greater equity, student achievement, and teacher preparedness in US schools. The center's research often is situated within classrooms and schools because of its view that this is of vital importance to any educational intervention.

The Consortium for School Networking (CoSN)
1025 Vermont Ave. NW, Ste. 1010, Washington, DC 20005
(202) 861-2676
e-mail: info@cosn.org
website: www.cosn.org

CoSN is an organization for K–12 educators who use technology strategically to improve teaching and learning. CoSN provides products and services to support leadership development, advocacy, coalition building, and awareness of emerging technologies.

Digital Media and Learning Research Hub (DML)
4000 Humanities Gateway, Irvine, CA 92697
(949) 824-8180
e-mail: dmlhub@hri.uci.edu
website: dmlcentral.net

The DML is dedicated to analyzing and interpreting the impact of the Internet and digital media on education, civic engagement, and youth. The organization investigates the ways in which digital technology is changing learning environments, social and civic institutions, and youth culture; works to support the growth of the emerging digital media and learning field and community; and spreads thought leadership and best practices for next generation learning and civics.

The George Lucas Educational Foundation (GLEF)
PO Box 3494, San Rafael, CA 94912
(415) 662-1600
e-mail: edutopia@glef.org
website: www.edutopia.org

GLEF was founded in 1991 as a nonprofit foundation to celebrate and encourage innovation in schools. It documents, disseminates, and advocates for exemplary programs in K–12 public schools to help these practices spread nationwide. It publishes the stories of innovative teaching and learning through a variety of media—a magazine, e-newsletters, DVDs, books, and its website.

International Society for Technology in Education (ISTE)
1710 Rhode Island Ave. NW, Ste. 900, Washington, DC 20036
(866) 654-4777
e-mail: iste@iste.org
website: www.iste.org

ISTE is a source for professional development, knowledge generation, advocacy, and leadership for innovation. A nonprofit membership organization, ISTE provides leadership and service to improve teaching, learning, and school leadership by advancing the effective use of technology in pre-K–12 classrooms and teacher education. Home of the National Educational Technology Standards (NETS), the Center for Applied Research in Educational Technology (CARET), and the National Educational Computing Conference (NECC), ISTE represents more than eighty-five thousand professionals worldwide.

National School Boards Association (NSBA)
Institute for the Transfer of Technology to Education (ITTE)
1680 Duke St., Alexandria, VA 22314
(703) 838-6722
e-mail: info@nsba.org
website: www.nsba.org

The NSBA established the Institute for the Transfer of Technology to Education (ITTE) in 1985 with its federation of state school boards associations. The mission of ITTE: Education Technology Programs advances NSBA's shared strategic vision that states, "Every school board will lead its community in preparing all students to succeed in a rapidly changing global society." ITTE is committed to engaging education, industry, and policy leaders to improve education processes and outcomes through knowledge and understanding of technology and organizational development. ITTE seeks to serve the many constituencies of NSBA through its involvement in national advocacy efforts, research, publications, meetings, and its school district membership program, the Technology Leadership Network.

Technology Student Association
1914 Association Dr., Reston, VA 20191-1540
(703) 860-9000
e-mail: general@tsaweb.org
website: www.tsaweb.org

The mission of the Technology Student Association is to prepare its membership for the challenges of a dynamic world by promoting technological literacy, leadership, and problem-solving skills, resulting in personal growth and opportunities.

BIBLIOGRAPHY

Books

Ann Bell, *Handheld Computers in Schools and Media Centers*. Worthington, OH: Linworth, 2007.

Susan J. Brooks-Young, ed. *Teaching with the Tools Kids Really Use: Learning with Web and Mobile Technologies*. Thousand Oaks, CA: Corwin Press, 2010.

Clayton M. Christensen, *Disrupting Class: How Disruptive Innovation Will Change the Way the World Learns*. New York: McGraw-Hill, 2011.

Liz Kolb, *Cell Phones in the Classroom: A Practical Guide for Educators*. Eugene, OR: International Society for Technology in Education, 2011.

Liz Kolb, *Toys to Tools: Connecting Student Cell Phones to Education*. Eugene, OR: International Society for Technology in Education, 2008.

Pamela Livingston, *1-to-1 Learning: Laptop Programs That Work*. 2nd ed. Eugene, OR: International Society for Technology in Education, 2009.

Lisa Nielsen, *Teaching Generation Text: Using Cell Phones to Enhance Learning*. San Francisco: Jossey-Bass, 2011.

Mark Pegrum, *From Blogs to Bombs: The Future of Digital Technologies in Education*. Crawley: University of Western Australia Press, 2009.

Will Richardson, *Blogs, Wikis, Podcasts, and Other Powerful Web Tools for Classrooms*. Thousand Oaks, CA: Corwin Press, 2010.

Periodicals and Internet Sources

Richard Byrne, "OMG! Texting in Class?," *School Library Journal*, March 2011.

Ed Finkel, "Should Districts Require Student-Owned Devices?," *District Administration*, October 2011.

Bryan Goodwin, "One-to-One Laptop Programs Are No Silver Bullet," *Educational Leadership*, February 2011.

Winnie Hu, "Math That Moves: Schools Embrace the iPad," *New York Times*, January 4, 2011.

Mike Kennedy, "Learning Tools: Schools Are Incorporating the iPad in Classrooms to Boost Performance," *American School and University*, June 2011.

Maclean's, "Don't Give Students More Tools of Mass Distraction," October 4, 2010.

Amber Marra, "Laptop Initiative in West Virginia Fizzles Out in Some Schools Where It Began," *Education Week*, April 27, 2011.

Josh McHugh, "Connecting to the 21st-Century Student," Edutopia. www.edutopia.org.

Cathleen Norris and Elliot Soloway, "One-to-One Computing Has Failed Our Expectations," *District Administration*, May 2010.

Tanya Roscorla, "The Impact of the iPad on K–12 Schools," *Converge*, February 9, 2011. www.convergemag.org.

Jeff Sovern, "Laptops in Class: How Distracting Are They?," *Christian Science Monitor*, June 6, 2011.

Kara Starr, "New Study Shows Laptops in Class May Hurt," *Flat Hat* (College of William and Mary), February 23, 2007.

Kenneth S. Trump, "Is It Safe to Allow Cell Phones in School?," *District Administration*, November/December 2009.

Audrey Watters, "Report Cards Are In: So Did the iPad in the Classroom Make the Grade?," Hack Education, January 18, 2011. www.hackeducation.com.

A
Angst, Corey M., 30, 31
Ash, Katie, 81

B
Baptiste, Lisa Jean, 23
Bernard, Ray, 83, 84
Bower, Jon, 43–44
bring-your-own-laptop
  programs
  are complicated but
    worthwhile, 46–53
  help education, 37–45
business partnerships, for
  school laptop programs, 53

C
cell phones/smartphones
  abuse of, during class is
    behavioral issue, 20, 62
  academic value of, 10–11
  advantages of iPods over, 28
  can be learning tools instead
    of distractions, 64–68
  in classrooms may lead to
    secretly created videos,
    74–80
  dictionary application, 12
  educational applications on,
    12–13
  percentage of teens allowed
    to carry in school/class, 66

percentage of youth owning,
  17–18, 19
schools should ban, 59–63
trial and error will produce
  best educational uses for, 22
Chambers, Becky, 26
Christian Science Monitor
  (newspaper), 9

D
Dede, Christopher, 18, 22
Department of Education, US,
  49
DiCello, Darren, 21
Di Chiro, Juli, 19–20
Distracted (Jackson), 71
Doherty, Richard, 42
Doty, David S., 86
DyKnow, 33

E
electronic communication,
  between teachers and
  students raises difficult issues,
  81–87
electronic devices
  can be useful learning tools,
    8–14
  more schools are encouraging
    use of, 15–23
  percentage of youth owning,
    17–18, 27

schools must sometimes provide, 44–45

Empire High School (Vail, AZ), 37–38, 39, 42–43

Escambia County Schools (FL), 39–42

Evens v. L.A. Unified School District (1999), 78

F

Federoff, Matt, 37–38, 42, 45

Ferriter, William M., 64

Filreis, Al, 9

First Amendment, 78

Flynn, Ann, 82

G

Gingold, Jessica, 16

Griswold, William G., 33

Guerrero, Sandra, 79

H

Haynes, Joyce P., 84, 87

Henke, Karen Greenwood, 42

Hines, Walker, 82–83

Hoffman, Frank A., 82

Honawar, Vaishali, 74

Houston Independent School District, Roberts v. (1990), 78

Huberman, Ron, 23

Hutton, Tom, 77

I

Internet

as academic tool, 10

percentage of homes with access to, 44

use among youth, by location, *40*

use of via smartphones, 42

iPads, *16*

can hinder teaching, 29–36

iPods, can help students learning, 24–28

It's Learning, 43

J

Jackson, Maggie, 71–72, 73

Jindal, Bobbie, 82

K

Kaiser Family Foundation, 17–18

Killalea, Laura, 70

Kolb, Liz, 5

L

laptops, *32, 52*

percentages of students using for distracting activities in class, *57*

should be banned from classrooms, 54–58

See also bring-your-own-laptop programs

L.A. Unified School District, Evens v. (1990), 78

M

Madan, Vineet, 32

Manchester, Bette, 50

Manderson, Don, 39–40, 41, 45

Manzo, Kathleen Kennedy, 24
Martin, Paul, 76
media players
    instruction for students on
        use of, 42
    percentage of youth owning,
        17–18
Menchhofer, Kyle, 20
Metcalf, Kevin, 80
Mikva Challenge, 16–17, 23
Miller, Terri, 87
Mong, Joyce, 75, 78

N
NCLB (No Child Left
    Behind), 49
New York Times (newspaper),
    48
No Child Left Behind
    (NCLB), 49, 50
Novak, Eric, 59

O
O'Donovan, Eamonn, 46
*One-to-One Computing
    Evaluation Consortium*
    (Concord Consortium), 50
opinion polls. *See* surveys

P
parent education
    on laptop programs, 52–53
    on schools' cellphone-use
        policies, 21
Pew Research Center's
    Internet & American Life
    Project, 18

Politis, Kathy, 28
Poll Everywhere (website),
    66–67
polls. *See* surveys
Prensky, Marc, 10, 11
privacy rights, of teachers, 78

Q
Quillen, Ian, 15

R
Reed, Robert H., 34, 35–36
Rehak, Jay, 75–76, 79
Rheingold, Harold, 9–10
Ringle, Martin, 32, 35, 36
*Roberts v. Houston Independent
    School District* (1990), 78
Rosenberg, Day, 8
Roswell High School
    (Roswell, GA), 24–28

S
Schad, Lenny, 21
school policies
    on cell phone use, 41–42,
        78–79
    challenge of changing
        technologies to, 86–87
    community stakeholders'
        needs should be addressed
        in, 51–53
    on electronic
        communication between
        teachers/students, 81–85
    problem of standardizing
        devices in setting, 42–43

schools
  must sometimes provide
    devices, 44–45
  should ban cell phones,
    59–63
Schuler, Mark, 24, 26–27
Scidmore, Robert, 18
Simon, Beth, 33, 34
Skinner, Georgianna, 44
Smart Mobs (Rheingold), 9
smartphones. *See* cell phones/
  smartphones
Snyder, Timothy, 54
software, educational
  effectiveness of, 49
  must be chosen to works on
    all devices, 43–44
  for tablet PCs, 33–34
Soloway, Elliot, 22
Spurka, Edward, 25
Steeves, Kevin, 43
Steinhaus, Paul, 29–30, 33
Strom, David, 75, 79
students
  electronic communication
    between teachers and, raises
    difficult issues, 81–87
  iPads may not benefit, 29–36
  iPods benefit, 24–28
  laptops are distraction for,
    56–58
  make final decision on
    educational tools, 34–36
  preparation for laptop
    programs, 51–52

surveys
  on home Internet access, 44
  on ownership of electronic
    devices among youth,
    17–18
  of teachers on technology
    and education, *11*

T
tablet PCs, 29, 35–36
  iPad vs, 30–31, *31*, 33–34
Taylor, Gord, 5
T.C. Williams High School
  (Alexandria, VA), 69–70,
  73
TDSB (Toronto District
  School Board), 59, 61–62
teachers
  electronic communication
    between students and, raises
    difficult issues, 81–87
  legal rights of, when secretly
    video-taped, 77
  need education on schools'
    cellphone-use policies, 21
  preparation for laptop
    programs, 51–52
  schools ignore embarrassing
    videos of, 77
  threat of secret videotaping
    to, 75–77
  views on technology and
    education, *11*
test scores, one-to-one laptop
  programs and, 47–50

text messaging/messages, *72*

  among teens, frequency of, by age, 70, 86

  annual numbers of in Canada, by year, *61*

  average number exchanged monthly, by gender/age group, *71*

  is a distraction from learning, 69–73

textbooks

  for iPads, limited availability of, 32–33

  netbooks *vs.*, 44–45

Thagard, Paul, 5

Thumann, Lisa, 28

Toronto District School Board (TDSB), 59, 61–62

Turkle, Sherry, 70–71

U

Ubiquitous Presenter (software program), 33, 34

V

Vasey, Michael, 33

W

Webb, Elizabeth, 28

Weinstock, Jeff, 37

Welsh, Patrick, 69

Wheeler, Thomas E., III, 78

Wieder, Ben, 29

Wright, John, 80

writing skills

  technology has improved, 9–10

  text messaging does not improve, 72, 73

Y

Yohey, Todd, 17, 18

YouTube, 10, 76, 79, 80

  video postings on, 74, 75, 77

  First Amendment and postings on, 78

Z

Zucker, Andrew, 50